The Web Conferencing IDEA BOOK

for Learning and Human Resources

Henry E. Liebling

Assisted by

Ruth Ann Forrester

For learning, training, talent management, and human resources professionals who want to have great, interactive, real-time meetings and training sessions, with people in different locations.
Less travel and less driving.

ISBN 978-0-9789159-3-3

Printed in United States of America

10 9 8 7 6 5 4 3 2 1

This book is based on the comprehensive (242 pages) *"The Web Conferencing Imperative for Collaboration, Productivity, and Training" by Henry E. Liebling.*

Published by Strategic Business and Technology Alliances, Inc.
3300 Hamilton Mill Road, Suite 102-PMB 135, Buford, GA 30519

Book cover design, custom illustrations, and desktop publishing by Ruth Ann Forrester,
Strategic Business and Technology Alliances, Inc.

Introduction

Web Conferencing is a *"Same Time, Different Place"* method of working. Web Conferencing brings people together who are in different locations.

Hundreds of IDEAS are presented for learning, training, and human resources professionals. Chapter 1 presents "the basics" about Web Conferencing. Chapter 2 gives "examples" and "case studies" for using Web Conferencing for interactive, engaging, and collaborative virtual meetings, and for distance and blended learning. Chapter 3 provides 65 additional insights to help you and your organization be successful with Web Conferencing.

In writing this book, I bring together two sets of experience. First, I am a seasoned training and development consultant and second, I began using software that enabled virtual meetings and distance learning in 1992.

I feel that Web Conferencing is an essential tool for anyone working in HR and Learning / Training. You can use Web Conferencing for *day-to-day operations*, *new initiatives*, *managing relationships*, and *adult learning*. To me, using this tool is as important as typing documents and using a cell phone and mobile device.

Whether you need to save time and expense associated with travel, or you want to work at your best with people in different location, or you want to help the environment, then Web Conferencing is a tool to learn more about and to more frequently use.

Sincerely,

Henry E. Liebling

Is Web Conferencing For You?

Instructions: Place a checkmark (✓) in the left column if the benefit statement in the right column is important to you.

	Cut travel expense and gasoline use and improve productivity.
	Reduce commute time.
	Improve coordination and collaboration with geographically distributed team members.
	Make better and faster decisions. Shorten cycle times. Be more nimble. (Experts and team members are located in distributed locations.)
	Close communications gaps between headquarters and field offices.
	Improve employee communications and increase employee connectedness.
	Enhance your supplier/partner relationships.
	Increase the effectiveness of remote meetings.
	Improve learning and performance.
	Develop/enhance your blended learning strategy.
	Get training developed and delivered more quickly.
	Quality of Life: Have more time for family and personal goals.

Use Web Conferencing to supplement and/or replace "in-person" meetings that require travel.

When your telephone calls and audio conferences would benefit by everyone "seeing the same thing," then use Web Conferencing.

How To Get Started With Web Conferencing

Develop a Web Conferencing Mindset

Here are several questions you and your staff can ask:

- Do I/we really have to travel to this meeting?
- How can we get that person's expertise into our team? (The person works in another building or hundreds/thousands of miles away.)
- What opportunities are we missing because of the distance factor?
- What telephone and conference calls would benefit by adding the "visual" component?

Here are several things to remember:

- The "visual" aspects of Web Conferencing are very powerful, for communications and learning.
- Each Web Conference can have its own style.
  - If you need to merely present content, do it.
  - If you need to co-create and/or interact and collaborate, then do that.
  - If you need to show a web page or software screens, then do that.
- Whether you lead a face-to-face meeting or a Web Conference virtual meeting or training class, planning and creativity can make things interesting for your audience.

How To Get Started With Web Conferencing, *continued*

Practice

A little practice builds your familiarity, confidence and skills.

- Get a practice buddy.
- If possible, practice on your own with two computers side-by-side. Connect them to the web and setup a Web Conference session.

Remember, with Internet connectivity, you can participate in Web Conferencing from anywhere.

How To Get Started With Web Conferencing, *continued*

Engaging and Involving Participants

I have discovered how powerful Web Conferencing is for interactive, collaborative virtual work, such as brainstorming, ideation, co-creating documents, defining a problem, building relationships, and reaching decisions. It's as if "asking questions" is more powerful than "telling."

Active Listening. One way to get the ball rolling is to demonstrate (model) and encourage "Active Listening." Active Listening behavior includes:

- Concentrate on the speaker.
- Focus on the information vs. your questions-reactions-responses or rebuttals.
- Ask questions to clarify your interpretation of what was said.

Use Questions to Involve. Another way to engage participants is to ask questions. I make an effort to think about the virtual meeting objectives and to prepare my questions ahead of time. Here are a few examples:

- *Regarding the last part of the discussion, what parts do you agree with? (Disagree with?)*
- *What steps would you take in dealing with this situation?*
- *From your point of view, what is the upside of Luisa's suggestion?*
- *Jane, if you accept Mike's suggestion, what impacts will that have on your organization? Bob, now that you've heard from Mike and Jane, what are your thoughts?*

Why Do We Have Web Conferences?

- ❑ Communicate
- ❑ Coordinate
- ❑ Collaborate
- ❑ Workforce
- ❑ Development

- ❑ Improve Employee Performance
- ❑ Plan
- ❑ Evaluate
- ❑ Disseminate Information (Webinar)

- ❑ Define a Problem
- ❑ Brainstorm
- ❑ Share Knowledge and Best Practices
- ❑ Inform
- ❑ Gain Insights from Others

- ❑ Project Management
- ❑ Build Relationships
- ❑ Make a Decision
- ❑ Build Consensus
- ❑ Edit/Revise Documents

- ❑ Lessons Learned (After a Project)
- ❑ Build a Solution
- ❑ See a Prototype
- ❑ Demo Software

- ❑ Sell Services and Products
- ❑ Open Up Lines of Communication
- ❑ Discuss Difficult Subjects
- ❑ Build a Hypothesis

When You Use Web Conferencing, You Help Reduce Traffic Congestion

When You Use Web Conferencing, You Help Reduce Gasoline Consumption

> ***"Congestion caused 3.7 billion hours of travel delay and 2.3 billion gallons of wasted fuel. If the current fuel prices are used, the congestion 'invoice' (costs) are about $65 billion."***
>
> Used with permission of:
> The 2005 Urban Mobility Report (2003 data)
> Texas Transportation Institute
> The Texas A&M University System

CONTENTS Page

Notes

Chapter 1

The Basics

Chapter Objectives

After reading this chapter, you are able to:

- Describe and discuss basic principles, terminology, capabilities, and benefits of Web Conferencing.
- Discuss what you can "see" and "change" during a Web Conference.
- Describe different "location" examples for different size Web Conferences.
- Make preliminary estimates of productivity gains.
- List ideas on how Web Conferencing can benefit you and your government organization.

What Is Web Conferencing?

Web Conferencing is an online, visual, voice and interactive collaborative technology that brings people together in **different locations at the same time.**

Web Conferencing is *also referred to as an online virtual meeting, synchronous real-time virtual meeting, or rich media web conference.*

I think of Web Conferencing as being interactive and *inter-locational* because it helps people get their work accomplished when they are not under the same roof.

Although Web Conferencing may include video communication, use of video is usually not the primary method.

Eleven (11) Important Things to Know About Web Conferencing

		Page
#1	Web Conferencing gives you an option of not traveling to a meeting or conference.	16
#2	Web Conferencing is easy and convenient. While online, use your computer, monitor, and keyboard.	17
#3	Everyone participates "at the same time." It brings people together (from 2 to 2000+) in different locations.	17
#4	Web Conferencing is visual. *"I see what you mean."* The adage, "*one picture is worth a thousand words*" is often true." (Visuals can enhance a conference or telephone call.)	33
#5	When presenting, the changes you make on your screen are seen by everyone at the same time.	38
#6	During a Web Conference, everyone "hears" what each other is discussing. *"I hear what you are saying."*	39
#7	Web Conferencing is used to increase the quantity and quality of communicating, coordinating, and collaborating.	39
#8	Web Conferencing is interactive, using built-in annotation tools.	40
#9	Web Conferencing increases productivity by reducing "lost time" associated with travel.	43
#10	Use Web Conferencing for ad hoc, planned, and regularly scheduled virtual meetings and training sessions.	45
#11	Web Conferencing is similar to traditional meetings.	46

#1. Web Conferencing gives you an option of not traveling to a meeting or conference.

With Web Conferencing, you don't "have to" travel to a meeting.

Blended Communications. In a typical day or week, you probably already blend your communications, using some form of telephone, e-mail, text chat, mobile communication device, and fax.

I encourage you to "add" Web Conferencing to the mix. It is powerful and affordable. Here are several examples of Blended Communications, as it relates to Web Conferencing.

	No Web Conferencing	With Web Conferencing
1	You use a car and/or airplane to travel to 50 meetings.	Use Web Conferencing for 25 meetings. Use a car and/or airplane for the other 25.
2	Your dispersed team sends documents around for review and comments in order to reach agreement. Time-consuming. Long cycle time.	Use Web Conferencing to more quickly build consensus. Reduce cycle time.
3	For a new initiative, the travel budget allows three face-to-face meeting over the next twelve months.	Web Conferencing allows the dispersed team to meet as often as they want.
4	You just got the word – no travel budget for the rest of the year. Ouch.	Step up the use of Web Conferencing to ensure your success.

#2. Web Conferencing is easy and convenient. While online, use your computer, monitor, and keyboard.

During a Web Conference, each participant is at his or her computer and online (connecting to your organization's intranet, a private network, or the Internet). You connect to a Web Conference from almost anywhere. For example:

- Home office
- At work (office, office cube
- At work (meeting room, conference room, cafeteria)
- Hotel Room, Conference Center, and Auditorium
- Another person's office
- Airport
- Coffee shop (using a wireless "hot spot")

#3. Everyone participates "at the same time." It brings people (from 2 to 2,000+) together in different locations at the same time.

Web Conferencing is referred to as "*synchronous*" communications, or "at the same time." Telephone calls, instant messaging, and face-to-face meetings are also synchronous.

Are you familiar with the term "*asynchronous*?" It generally means "not at the same time." Examples: e-mail, fax, voice mail, postal mail, overnight mail, and online workrooms.

The next page contains an "At The Same Time" chart, for twenty-seven cities in fifteen countries.

On pages 19 - 32, please find examples of using Web Conferencing between different locations, for different size virtual meetings and learning.

You should verify the exact time for a city. For example, the time of the year can impact the location's time.

Global Clock - At The Same Time *Verify these times*		
5 am	Honolulu, HI	USA
7 am	Juneau, AK	USA
8 am	Salem, OR San Francisco, CA Simi Valley, CA	USA USA USA
9 am	Boise, ID Denver, CO Calgary, Alberta	USA USA Canada
10 am	Austin, TX Little Rock, AR Topeka, KS Mexico City	USA USA USA Mexico
11 am	Atlanta, GA Boston, MA Washington, DC Santiago	USA USA USA Chile
4 pm	London	England, U.K.
5 pm	Brussels Oslo Pretoria Tel Aviv Warsaw	Belgium Norway So. Africa Israel Poland
6 pm	Baghdad	Iraq
7 pm	Moscow	Russia
11 pm	Shanghai	China
Midnight	Tokyo	Japan
1 am (next day)	Sydney, New South Wales	Australia

Exact Time – World Clocks
http://www.timeanddate.com
http://www.worldtimeserver.com

Example 1-1: 2 people

Locations	Explanation
A & B	▪ Each person is at computer. ▪ Each person needs a telephone or headset and microphone in order to listen and speak to the other person.

Example 1-2: 4 people

Locations	Explanation
A	▪ Person uses a headset.
B	▪ Person uses a traditional telephone. ▪ Person uses a webcam to show a headshot of him speaking.
C	▪ Two people "buddy up" and use the same computer. This could be significant if your Web Conferencing software has a limit of the number of licenses or subscription seats. ▪ They use a desktop speakerphone to speak and to listen to the others. ▪ They use a webcam on top of the monitor. They manually move it to focus on one person at a time.

Example 1-3: 10 people

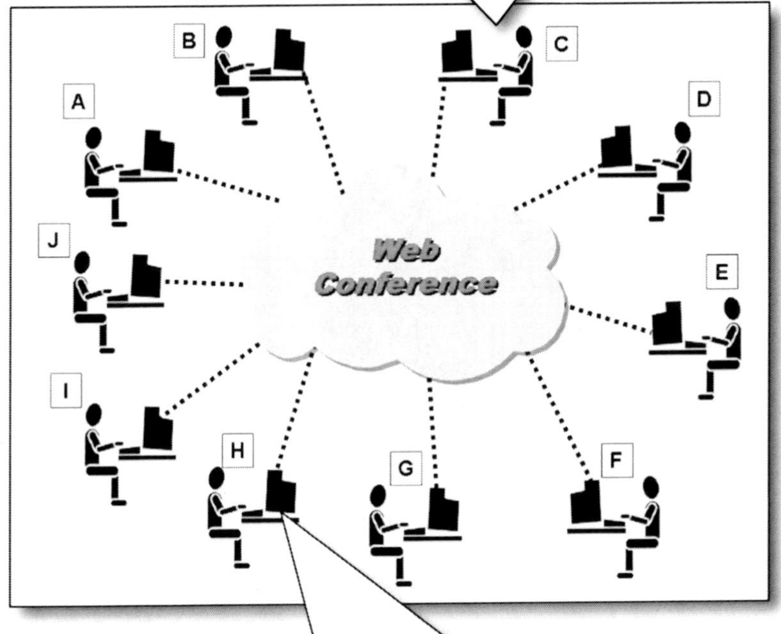

Locations	Explanation
All Locations	▪ Each person is at computer. ▪ Each person also needs a telephone or headset and microphone, so they can listen and speak to each other. Note: In this illustration, no one uses a webcam.

Example 1-4: 50 people

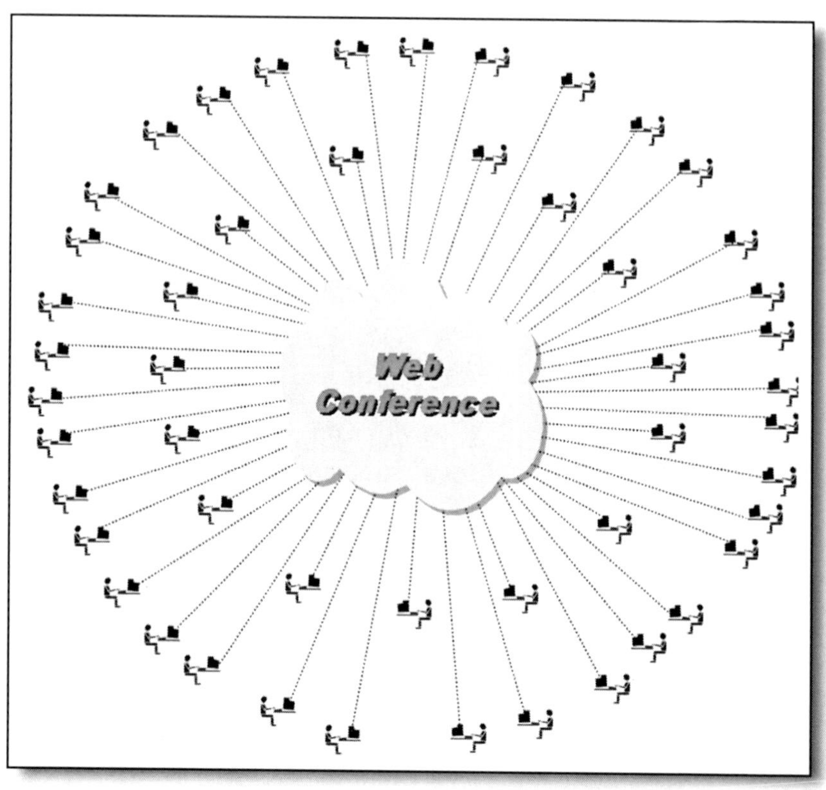

Locations	Explanation
All	▪ Each person is at computer. ▪ Each person also needs a telephone or headset and microphone, which allows them to listen and speak with each other. Note: In this illustration, no one is using a webcam, but they could be. Tip: Because of the size, you probably want to disable (turn off) annotation tools for everyone.

Room Equipment for Examples 1-5 and 1-6:

The next two examples show people participating in a Web Conference with people connecting from individual computers and also from a computer in a small conference room. In order to make these Web Conferences work, you need the following:

Web or Internet Connection and Computer: The small meeting rooms need to connect to the Web or Internet, so the computer can connect to the other people in the Web Conference.

Speakerphone: Since sound is important, you need to have a speakerphone in each meeting room. Make sure you have a speakerphone that can accommodate the number of people in the room and how far away they are from the speakerphone.

Projection System: The computer is connected to a device (e.g. LCD projector) that projects images on the computer's small monitor, onto the large projection screen. Some people use portable projectors; others use ceiling-mounted units.

Electronic Whiteboard: The computer is connected to the electronic whiteboard (also known as a "digital whiteboard"). What you write on the electronic whiteboard immediately appears on individual computers and other electronic whiteboards and projection systems. In addition, what you display on a PC is shown on the electronic whiteboard.

Room Technology for Collaboration

"Room Technology" keeps getting better. Look for products in the following categories: virtual environment systems, visual display products, interactive real-time visual display systems, videoconferencing and telepresence equipment.

Room Technology Examples

Projection Systems

Room Technology

Electronic Whiteboard

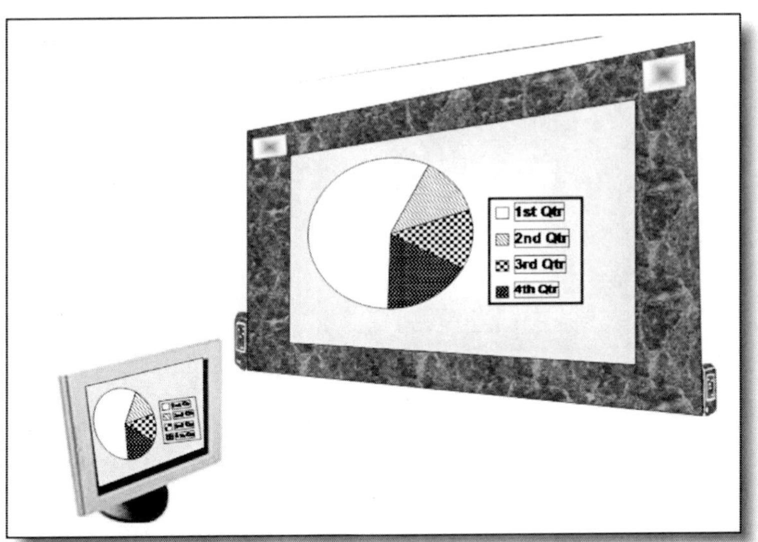

Speakerphone

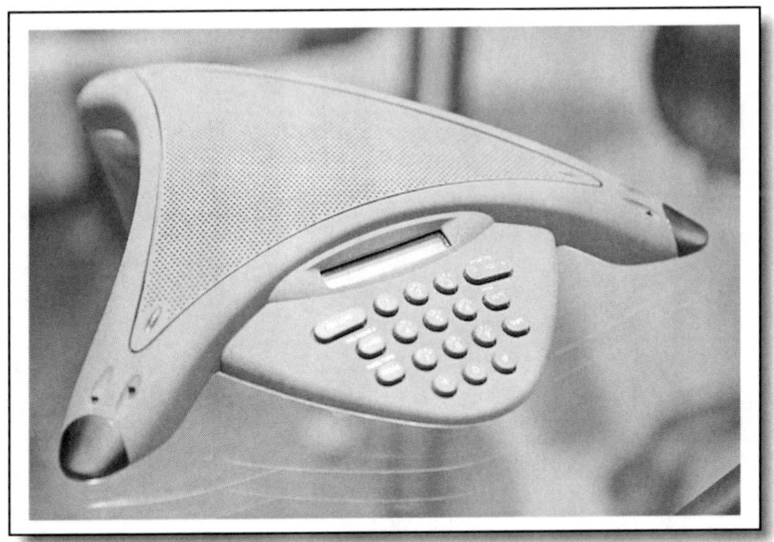

Example 1-5: 26 participants

Locations	Explanation
A	▪ Person is a Co-Presenter. ▪ Traditional telephone or VoIP (voice over Internet Protocol) is also used for the audio (voice) part of the Web Conference.
B	▪ 14 people are in a small meeting room. ▪ 1 Co-Presenter who also fields local questions and responds to questions from the others.
C	▪ 7 participants in a small meeting room. ▪ 1 person in the role of "Room Coordinator." This person fields local questions and coordinates these questions with B.
D	▪ Two SMEs (subject matter experts) use the same computer and a desktop speakerphone and webcam.
B & C	▪ Computer is connected to a projection system. ▪ Speakerphone or speaker system is used for the audio.

Example 1-6: 66 participants

Locations	Explanation
A, B, C	▪ Each person is at computer. ▪ Traditional telephone or VoIP is also used for the audio (voice) part of the Web Conference.
D	▪ Primary Presenter is in this room.
E & F	▪ Room Coordinator provides assistance, especially in fielding local questions.
D, E, F	▪ Each conference room has 20 participants. ▪ Computer is connected to a projection system. ▪ There is at least one speakerphone in each room.

Room Equipment for Examples 1-7 through 1-10:

The next four examples depict Web Conferences utilizing large rooms, such as auditoriums, conference rooms, hotel ballrooms, and lecture halls.

In order to make these Web Conferences work, you need the following:

Web or Internet Connection and Computer: These large rooms need to connect to the Web or Internet.

Projection Systems and/or Electronic Whiteboards: Everyone needs to "see." For these larger Web Conferences, you may want to use several projection systems and/or electronic whiteboards.

Sound System: So that everyone in the large rooms can "hear" the same message, you need to use a sound system. Remember, the sound system in one large room needs to "connect" to the sound system in the other large rooms.

Microphones: Here are several ways in which microphones are used in these larger rooms:

- The Room/Auditorium Presenter uses a microphone to project his or her voice to people in all the rooms.

- A microphone is available for the participants. This allows them to express themselves to the people in their room/auditorium.

Depending on the design of your Web Conference, you may or may not want the participants in one large room to be able to hear what participants are saying in other large rooms.

Example 1-7: 200+ people

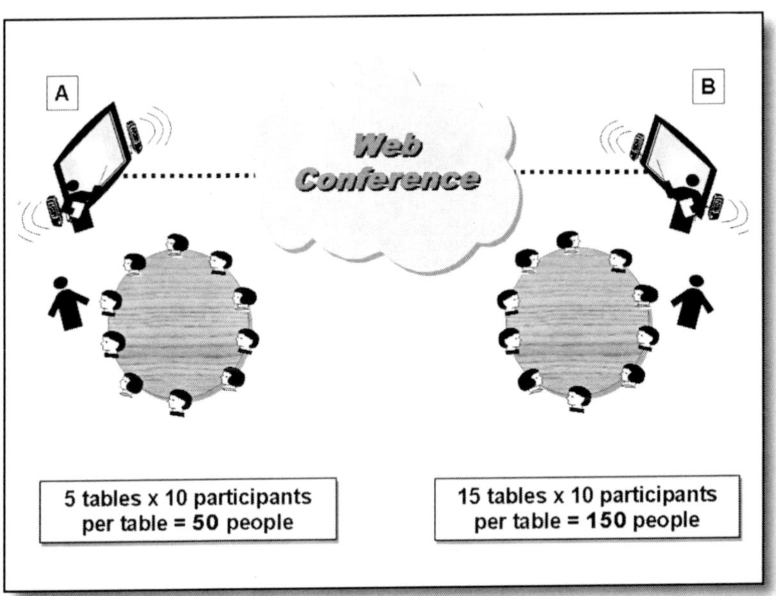

Locations	Explanation
A	▪ 50 people, sitting 10 participants at a table. ▪ Several people in the role of Conference Room Coordinator for the "breakout" activities. ▪ One person is Co-Presenter. People in B can hear the Co-Presenter.
B	▪ 150 people, sitting 10 participants at a table. ▪ Several people in the role of Conference Room Coordinator for the "breakout" activities. ▪ One person is Co-Presenter. People in A can hear the Co-Presenter.
A & B	▪ Each conference room uses multiple large projection systems and/or electronic whiteboards connected to a computer. ▪ Each room has an appropriate sound system. ▪ Several microphones are passed around the conference room; this allows the participants to easily hear each other's questions and comments.

Example 1-8: 307 people

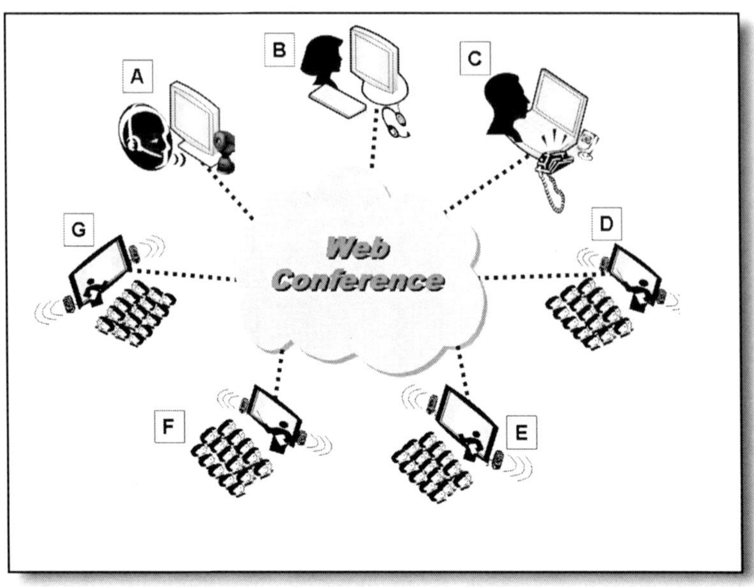

Locations	Explanation
A, B, C	▪ Each person is at his or her own computer. ▪ Each person also needs a voice connection. ▪ A & C have webcams at their desk.
D, E, F, & G	▪ Each conference room has 75 participants. ▪ Each has appropriate sound system and computer. ▪ Each uses an Electronic Whiteboard. What is written or annotated at one whiteboard shows up on the other whiteboards and computer screens.
D & F	▪ Both have a Co-Presenter or Co-Facilitator.
E & G	▪ Both have a Room Coordinator to handle local questions.

Example 1-9: 400+ people

Locations	Explanation
A & B	▪ The Co-Presenters are at their own computer.
C	▪ Large lecture hall with 250 people.
D	▪ Large lecture hall with 150 people.
C & D	▪ Each large lecture room uses multiple large projection systems connected to a computer. ▪ Each has an appropriate sound system allowing everyone to hear the Co-Presenters. ▪ A Room Coordinator is in each of the large lecture halls. This person "is the voice" when speaking for the people in C and D. ▪ Additional Room Coordinators are used for crowd control and coordination of handouts. ▪ Several microphones are used for the participants.

<u>Example 1-10</u>: 1,200+ people

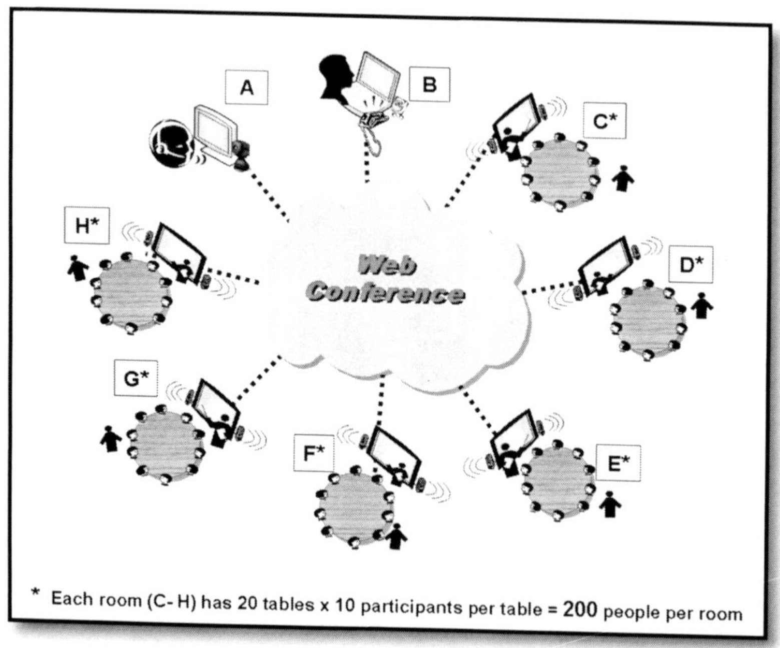

* Each room (C- H) has 20 tables x 10 participants per table = **200** people per room

Locations	Explanation
A & B	▪ The Co-Presenters. Each connects from their computer and uses a webcam. ▪ A uses a headset. B uses a traditional phone.
C, D, E, F, G & H	▪ Six very large conference rooms, with 200 hundred people in each, sitting 10 at a table. ▪ Each large room uses multiple large projection systems/electronic whiteboards connected to a computer. ▪ Each uses a sound system which allows everyone to hear the Co-Presenters. Microphones are also used. ▪ One person is the Master Coordinator for each of the large lecture rooms. This person "is the voice" when speaking for the people in the rooms. ▪ Additional Room Coordinators are used for "breakout" activities.

#4. Web Conferencing is visual. *"I see what you mean."* The adage, *"one picture is worth a thousand words"* is often true.

During a Web Conference, all of the participants "see" the same visual content on their own computer's monitor at the same time. During the Web Conference, you can switch between what you see. This is similar to the behavior in a traditional face-to-face meeting, when you might use a whiteboard, slide presentation, text document, and project plan during the same meeting.

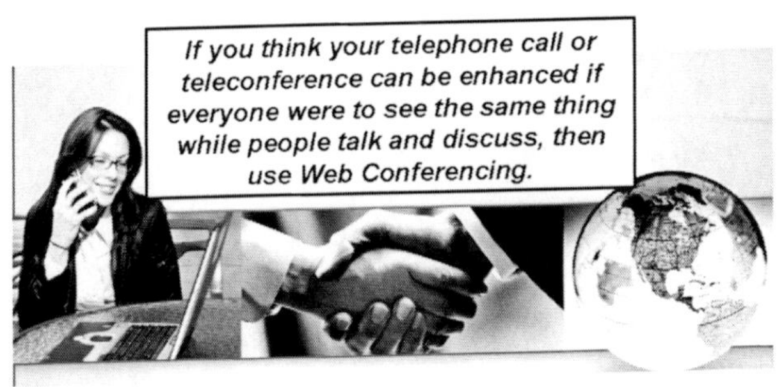

What Everyone Sees During a Web Conference

Whether you use software from Microsoft®, OpenOffice.org, Corel®, Mindjet®, Kidasa Software, Inc., and others, you can show the software screens to other people from your computer.

Text Documents (Word Processed Documents)

Use your word processing program for:

- Vendor Contracts and Statements of Work
- Memos, Reports, Studies, and Change Management Plans
- Organizational Staffing Plans and Organizational Charts
- Employee Recruitment Ads and On-boarding Steps
- Program Plans and Project Charter
- Lesson Objectives, Story Boards, Instructional Design, and Course Materials
- Employee Benefit Marketing Materials

What Everyone Sees During A Web Conference, *continued*

Financial Information

Use your spreadsheet program for:

- Financial Reports
- Monthly and Program Expenditure Reports
- Department, Program, and Project Budget Analysis
- Vendor Purchases, month-to-month
- Budgets

Slide Presentations

Use your presentation program for:

- Slides on any subject

Project Plans and Timelines

Use your project management application for:

- Project Maps and Phases
- Project Tasks and Sub-Tasks
- Estimated Task Durations
- Resource Groups
- Material Resources
- Reports

Whiteboards, Process Maps, and Brainstorming Diagrams

Use your diagramming and business graphics software for:

- Ideas
- Process Flow Charts
- Fishbone and Force Field Analysis Diagrams
- Mind Maps
- Templates

What Everyone Sees During a Web Conference, *continued*

Web Sites

- Look at your organization's intranet
- View public web sites

Desktop and Web Applications

- Human Resources Information Systems
- Learning Portal and LMS and LCMS screens
- Geographic Information System (GIS) screens
- Performance Management System
- Data Bases
- Time Sheet Applications
- Expense Reimbursement Software
- eCommerce and eProcurement Applications
- ERP (Enterprise Resource Planning), CRM (Customer Relationship Management), Supply Chain, Materials Management, and so forth
- Network Monitoring Software
- Security Systems

Pictures and Images

Anything digitized, such as:

- Still Photos (digitized)
- Architectural Plans
- Facilities & Buildings
- Redevelopment Properties
- Topography Maps

Video images

- Video "talking head" of Web Conferencing Presenter or Participant
- Video movies embedded in a slide presentation

Do I need a web camera (webcam)?

You do not need a webcam to participate in a Web Conference. However, using a webcam to "show your face" to the other participants adds a nice touch of "socialization" to the Web Conference.

What Everyone Sees During A Web Conference, *continued*

Meeting Agenda

Talent Management

- Recruitment
- On-Boarding
- Employee Retention

Financial Report

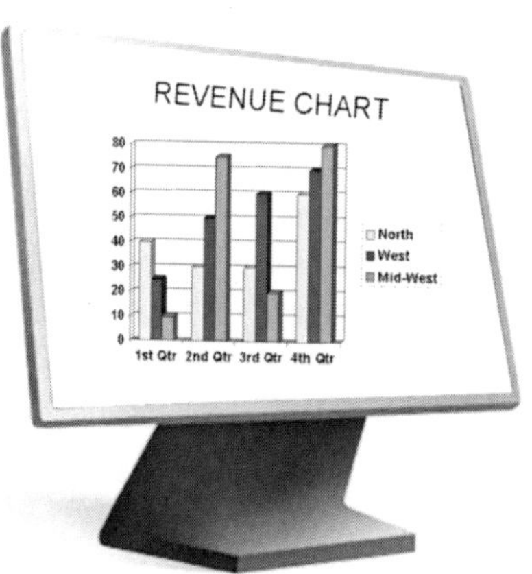

Business Process Flow Chart

Text Document

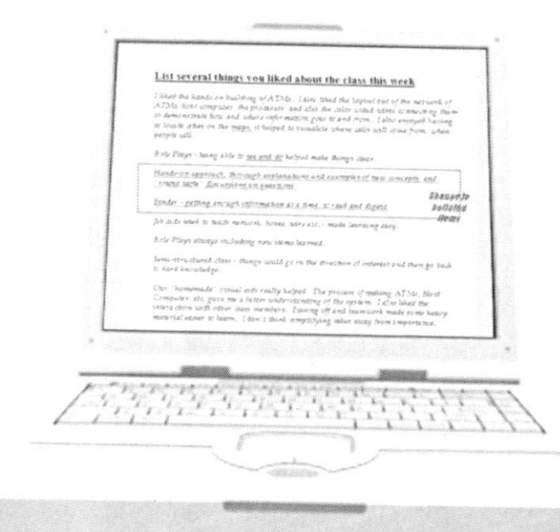

What Everyone Sees During a Web Conference, *continued*

Project Management

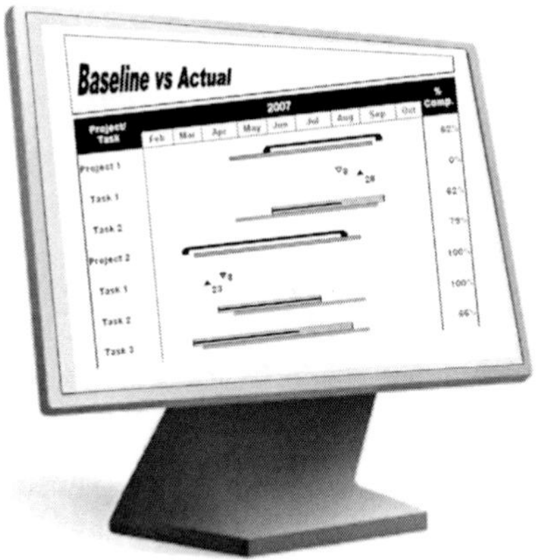

Web Site or Portal

Digital Aerial Images

Hosted Software

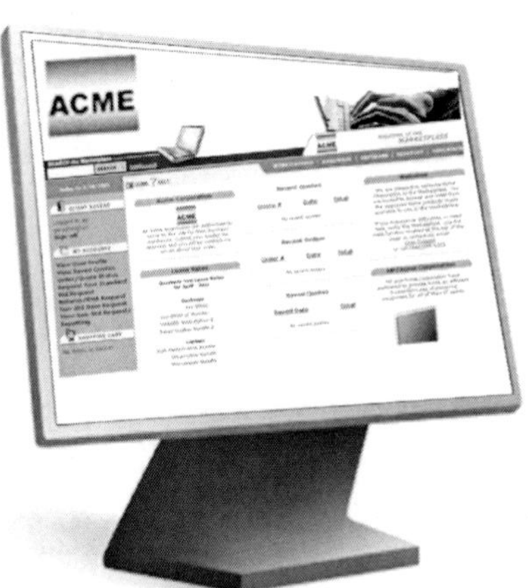

Project Management Image by permission of Kidasa Software, Inc.

Digital Aerial Image by permission of Pictometry International Corp.

#5. When presenting, the changes you make on your screen are seen by everyone at the same time.

This is a powerful capability of Web Conferencing. When you make a "real-time" change to what is on your screen, everyone immediately sees it. This feature can stimulate very interesting discussions, brainstorming, new ideas, debates, and agreements. There is more on this point, starting on page 41, titled "Screen Sharing / Application Sharing." *Here are several examples*:

- **You have a text document or presentation slide up on the screen**. During the Web Conference, you make changes to it; you add in or take out something. Everyone sees the changes, which drives discussion and/or agreements.

Co-create a document, starting from scratch.
Collaborate on a "draft" document.
Co-edit a "draft" document before it becomes "Final."
Use for analysis and data collection. For example, when completing a "Force-Field Analysis." Bring up a two-column document. Type in "Restraining Forces" (left column) and "Driving Forces" (right column) as the participants verbalize them.

- **You show a financial spreadsheet**. During the Web Conference, you type changes in the spreadsheet cells. Instantly, this creates a different financial picture for everyone to see and discuss. This is powerful if you need to discuss various "what if" financial scenarios for a project or plan.

- **You show a portal, web site, or software application to everyone**. While it is seen by everyone, you click on links and/or type into it. As you click on the links and/or type, everyone sees how the web site or application behaves.

#6. During a Web Conference, everyone "hears" what each other is discussing.

"I hear what you are saying."

In addition to being able to "see" the same things during a Web Conference, the participants **"speak" and "listen"** to each other.

#7. Web Conferencing is used to increase the quantity and quality of communicating, coordinating, and collaborating.

One of the things I consistently experience with Web Conferencing is that people become acclimated to it relatively quickly. People have said to me, *"I actually stopped thinking I was not in the same physical room because we were clicking together so well."* Others have said, *"It is easier to co-create."*

Once the acclimation occurs, people get on with their business, which involves some type of *communicating, coordinating*, and *collaborating*.

Some Web Conferencing systems allow you to "pass control" to other people in the Web Conferencing. Suppose, for example, you initiate the Web Conference. You start out by showing and leading a discussion about the *content on your computer screen.* During the Web Conference, you "pass control" to another participant, who shows everyone the *content on his or her computer*. This is a powerful technique for your team.

#8. Web Conferencing is interactive, using built-in annotation tools.

Web Conferencing has built-in "*interactivity tools*" (*annotation* or *markup tools*) you use with your mouse and keyboard.
During a Web Conference, use these tools to communicate and to "mark up" what you see on the computer screen. These tools help overcome the reality that you are not face-to-face. Using these tools makes your Web Conferences more social, engaging, and interesting. <u>*Here are a few examples*</u>:

Mark-up

- This tool is like writing on a white board or easel pad. Or, marking up a diagram and distributing it to everyone. Use your mouse to circle or highlight a key word or phrase you want everyone to focus on.

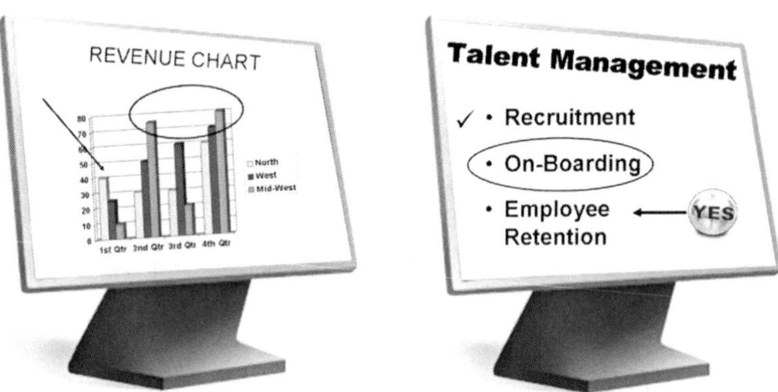

Hand Raising

- Some systems allow you to use your mouse to designate that you are raising your hand. *("Hey, call on me.")*

Text Chat

- An advantage of using a keyboard text chat tool (built into the Web Conferencing software or with an external instant messaging system) during a Web Conference is you can *send* and *respond* to others without interrupting the "verbal flow of the meeting. Some systems give you the flexibility of sending "private chats" (to just one person) and "public chats" (to everyone).

Polls and Surveys

- These tools allow the Web Conferencing Leader and Web Conferencing Presenter(s) to get participant feedback on a question, or questions. Using a poll or survey is similar to what you might already be doing in a face-to-face meeting, when you give this instruction to the participants, *"If you agree with such and such, please raise your hand."*

- If your Web Conferencing system has this feature, it may allow you to set up your question(s) in "True/False," "Yes/No," or "Multiple Choice" formats.

Screen Sharing / Application Sharing

- Screen Sharing / Application Sharing allows someone in the Web Conference, often the Presenter or Leader, to "show" (share) an application that is on his or her hard drive. Using this tool makes it possible for the other participants "see" the application at the same time.

> ***"Let's app share this ..."***
>
> Sometimes you hear a person say, *"Let's app share that out to the team*" which means they want to use Web Conferencing to show/share something to people in other locations.

Screen Sharing / Application Sharing, *continued*

- What's cool is the "other people" do not need to have the application on their hard drive. For example, if the Web Conferencing Leader is showing and discussing a Project Plan to the team, the other team members do not have to have the project planning software on their computer.

- Screen Sharing / Application Sharing also enables, for example, the Web Conferencing Presenter, to share an application with everyone else and then MAKE CHANGES to it.

  Within a few seconds or less, everyone else in the Web Conference sees what those changes are. If this is a bit confusing, think of it this way. You are at your computer and a colleague is standing behind you watching what you type. As you type into the application, both you and your colleague see what is being typed. The same thing occurs with Web Conferencing. Everyone sees the changes as you type them.

- Co-creating: This is a great feature for editing and co-creation (courseware, presentation slides for a key stakeholder, or a RFP or contract). When everyone agrees *at the same time*, it is faster than sending documents around (back and forth) for feedback and agreement.

- Financial spreadsheet: When discussing the details contained in a financial spreadsheet, someone can type in the spreadsheet cells to change the numbers. Everyone sees the changes at the same time. This fosters dialogue for "what if" scenarios.

- Human Resources. With a HR information system (or other system), you type into the fields, click the continue button (of the software application), and the next software screen is seen by everyone. You can do the same with web portals, LCMS, LMS, and so forth.

#9. Web Conferencing increases productivity by reducing "lost time" associated with travel.

Lost Time

I think of "lost time" as just that. Time "lost" because you are "just sitting" in automobile traffic or "sitting" at the airport, while traveling to a meeting or conference.

The opportunity with Web Conferencing is to Reduce "Lost Time" (associated with travel) and Gain "New Time."

As Time Management Guru Alan Lakein wrote in How to Get Control of Your Time and Your Life, it is important to make choices on what you do with your time. **Wouldn't it be awesome to have some New Time in your life ?!?!**

The following charts give you an idea of the "New Time" you gain when you reduce "Lost Time" associated with traveling to and from meetings and training sessions.

IF	THEN
1 person saves three hours per week, because you are not traveling,	this person will have over 150 hours of "**New Time**" in a year (450 hours in 3 years)
100 people save three hours per week, because they are not traveling,	your organization will have 15,000 hours of "**New Time**" in a year. (45,000 hours in 3 years)
1000 people save three hours per week, because they are not traveling,	your organization will have 150,000 hours of "**New Time**" in a year. (450,000 hours in a 3 years)

How would you use this New Time?

New Time – It Adds Up!

When You Reduce Travel by	One Person New Time You Gain		
	Each Month	Yearly	3 Years
30 minutes per day	10 hrs.	120 hrs.	360 hrs.
1 hour per day	20 hrs.	240 hrs.	720 hrs.
2 hours per day	40 hrs.	480 hrs.	1,440 hrs.
5 hours per week	20 hrs.	240 hrs.	720 hrs.
10 hours per week	40 hrs.	480 hrs.	1,440 hrs.

When You Reduce Travel by	100 People New Time for 100 People		
	Each Month	Yearly	3 Years
30 minutes per day	1,000 hrs.	12,000 hrs.	36,000 hrs.
1 hour per day	2,000 hrs.	24,000 hrs.	72,000 hrs.
2 hours per day	4,000 hrs.	48,000 hrs.	144,000 hrs.
5 hours per week	2,000 hrs.	24,000 hrs.	72,000 hrs.
10 hours per week	4,000 hrs.	48,000 hrs.	144,000 hrs.

When You Reduce Travel by	500 People New Time for 500 People		
	Each Month	Yearly	3 Years
30 minutes per day	5,000 hrs.	60,000 hrs.	180,000 hrs.
1 hour per day	10,000 hrs.	120,000 hrs.	360,000 hrs.
2 hours per day	20,000 hrs.	240,000 hrs.	720,000 hrs.
5 hours per week	10,000 hrs.	120,000 hrs.	360,000 hrs.
10 hours per week	20,000 hrs.	240,000 hrs.	720,000 hrs.

Adapted from "Handbook for Personal Productivity" by Henry E. Liebling.

#10. Use Web Conferencing for ad hoc, planned, and regularly scheduled virtual meetings and training sessions*.

Web Conferencing fits the way we normally do our meetings.

Ad **<u>hoc</u>** **Virtual Meetings and Learning and Training Sessions – at a moment's notice**

- In the course of a day, use Web Conferencing as many times as necessary, at a moment's notice.

<u>Planned</u> **Virtual Meetings and Learning and Training Sessions**

- We also have our planned meetings and training sessions. For planned virtual meetings and training sessions, people generally use e-mail, common calendaring systems, and instant messaging to establish the Web Conference's date and time.

<u>Regularly Scheduled</u> **Virtual Meetings and Learning and Training Sessions**

- Do you have a regular meeting, for example, every Tuesday morning? Do you have a regular "lunch and learn" on the first and third Wednesday of each month?

> * When Web Conferencing is used for training, it is often referred to in different ways, such as:
>
> - Virtual Classroom
> - Virtual Instructor-Led Classroom
> - Synchronous Virtual Classroom

#11. Web Conferencing is similar to traditional meetings.

This section highlights some of the *roles* and *tasks* that are performed during a Web Conference. Many of these roles and tasks are probably familiar to you already.

One Person Might Wear Multiple Hats

One person often performs multiple roles and tasks, especially for small Web Conferences. For example, one person wears the following hats:

WC (Web Conference) Leader: sets agenda and determines who needs to participate.

WC (Web Conference) Coordinator: sends out the Web Conferencing invitations.

WC (Web Conference) Presenter: gives a presentation or serves as a subject matter expert (SME).

Other roles may include:

- Web Conference **Designer** – "design" of the virtual meeting
- Web Conference **Attendees** or **Participants**
- Web Conferencing **Technical Support**
- **Instructional Design** for Virtual Synchronous Classroom Learning
- **Virtual Instructor** using Web Conferencing
- **IT Support**

Web Conferencing is an essential real-time, interactive tool for dispersed organizations.

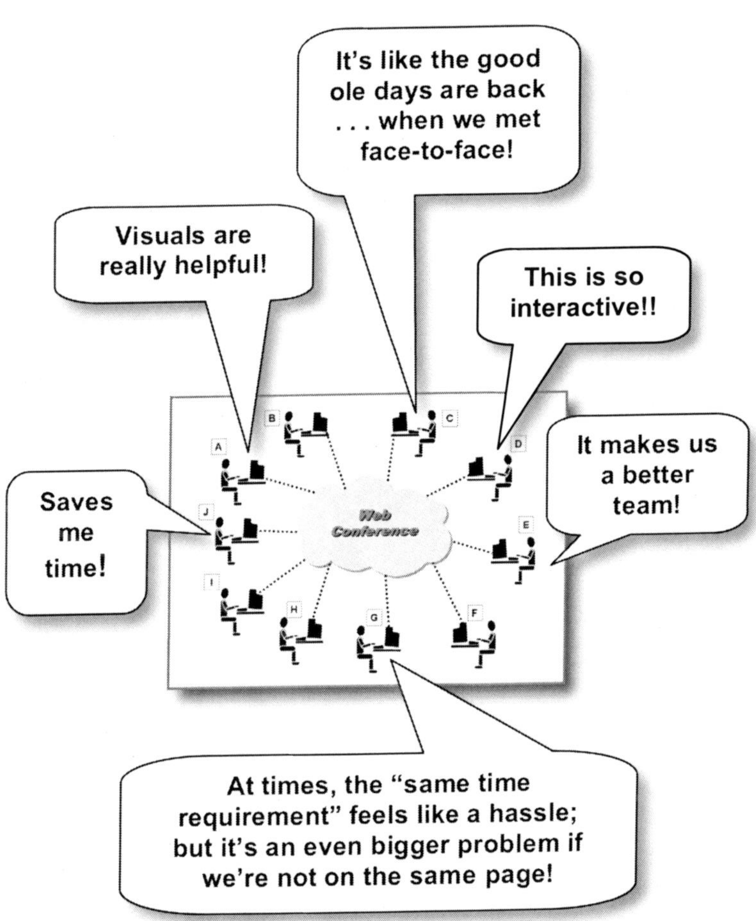

Notes

Chapter 2

Ideas

Chapter Objectives

After reading this chapter, you are able to:

- Identify Web Conferencing Case Studies that point out opportunities for you and your organization.
- Describe how to manage time, content, and involvement during a Web Conference.
- State and discuss ideas for designing and leading Web Conferences.

Web Conferencing IDEAS

This IDEAS chapter provides "mini" case studies, ideas, and examples of using Web Conferencing to accomplish your work with people in different locations. The chapter is organized into four broad areas of work:

- Day-To-Day Operations and Management
- New Initiatives
- Managing Relationships
- Learning and Training

I have provided context information, covering the case study's problem, goals, frequency of meeting, participants, and behavioral considerations.

As you read these, you will get ideas on the flow of a Web Conference. This includes content, process, roles, tasks (actions), interactions, and times. The times provided are estimates. Generally, an intact work team that is experienced with Web Conferencing gets up and running in just a few minutes.

Toward the back of this IDEAS chapter, you will find six examples of Blended Learning Processes.

Case Studies and Examples		Page

Use Web Conferencing for Day-To-Day Operations and Management

Use Web Conferencing virtual meetings to help you with these activities:

- ☐ Project status reviews, e.g. on recruitment, new employee on-boarding process, and work-at-home policy.
- ☐ Conducting budget reviews.
- ☐ Administering the diversity program.
- ☐ Involving dispersed experts when there is a crisis.
- ☐ Staff meetings.
- ☐ Having a collaborative discussion and reaching agreement with a peer or internal customer.
- ☐ Seeing intranet/portal updates and then giving feedback and approval.
- ☐ Employee benefits meetings – large audience.
- ☐ Employee relations.

What is the purpose of your Web Conference?

Do you need to achieve a high level of collaboration, interaction, and/or co-creation?

Or, do you need to inform the participants with new information, accompanied by light Q&A?

Knowing your purpose, helps ensure that Web Conferencing serves your needs.

2-1: Reports

Problem: The dispersed team was getting complaints about not getting reports out in a timely manner. Managing different points of view and sending documents back and forth and back and forth was eating up a lot of time.

Opportunity: Use Web Conferencing to decrease cycle time and complaints.

Frequency: As needed.

Participants: 2-10 people, who have worked together before.

Behavioral: Robust collaborative discussion followed by agreements. Participants see and discuss the document that everyone sees on their computer. They see the changes as they are made in real time.

15 minutes to 2 hours – Content and Process
2 - 5 minutes ▪ Web Conferencing Leader confirms that everyone can "see" and "hear."
0 – 10 minutes ▪ Socialization.
10 – 90 minutes ▪ Web Conferencing Leader opens the draft memo (text document) which everyone sees. ▪ Going from page to page, they have solid give-and-take discussions. They agree on changes to ideas, words and flow of the document. ▪ As changes are agreed to, Leader types in the text document. People see the changes as they are made.
3 -15 minutes ▪ Wrap up and Next Steps.

2-1: Reports, *continued*

Web Conferencing is an excellent tool when working on documents with people who are not under the same roof as you.

- Co-Create in Real-Time
- Edit and Revise in Real-Time
- Reach Agreements in Real-Time

Here are a few examples of what you can work on together:

- Project Plans, Alignment Reports/Diagrams, Business Processes Workflow Diagrams, Budgets, and Organizational Charts

- Recruitment Analysis, Talent Management Report, Succession Planning Study, Job Descriptions, and On-Boarding Program Description

- Memos, Speeches, Press Releases, Presentation Slides, Internal Marketing Materials, and Meeting Minutes

- Software Screens – from HR Portal, Web Site Pages, Learning Portal, LMS, LCMS, ERP, HR Mgt. Information System

- Course Learning Objectives and Instructional Designs

- Course Materials – Traditional Classroom, eLearning, and Synchronous Virtual Classroom

- Instructor Guides and Train-The-Trainer materials

- Detailed Agenda for an Offsite or Conference

- Performance Appraisal forms

- RFP Documents

2-2: Staff Meetings

Problem: Extended team members in multiple locations felt disconnected from each other and the department's overall strategy and operations.

Opportunity: Use Web Conferencing to socialize, to exchange information on activities and projects, and to better understand how they can help each other.

Frequency: Bi-weekly or monthly.

Participants: People who work together in six locations.

Behavioral: Team members socialize, welcome new members, view a variety of documents, exchange information, and have light collaborative discussions.

2 hours – Content and Process
5 minutes ▪ Web Conferencing Leader (department head) confirms that everyone can "see" and "hear." ▪ Web Conferencing Leader opens a text document to show the agenda. ▪ Randy volunteers to take minutes and record hot issues.
15 minutes ▪ Socialization. Unstructured chit-chat. Some participants show JPG pictures of vacation, hobby, and family. ▪ Luisa announces that it is Susie's birthday.

continue to next page

2-2: Staff Meetings, *continued*

<table>
<tr><td>40 minutes
▪ Nazim shows the monthly financial report. Leads Q&A.
▪ Carlos shows a Training Module Revision chart. It contains due dates, responsible person or vendor, and known issues. Light discussion and questions.
▪ Deion and Inger show and navigate around the intranet site. It is being revised for the new HR employee performance program. Robust discussion and Q&A.</td></tr>
<tr><td>Break - 10 minutes</td></tr>
<tr><td>40 minutes
▪ Omar and Latanya show the Train-The-Trainer outline. Minimum discussion.
▪ Joel and George show documents about and discuss the upcoming community volunteer program.
▪ Aki gives a slide presentation on the proposed Internal Marketing program. She also shows the marcom calendar.
▪ Luisa, Geneva, and Alana give a presentation on the proposed Blended Learning initiative. Robust discussion.
▪ Department head shows a 3-slide presentation that is to be given to the company president. Asks for volunteers to build it out to 10-slides.</td></tr>
<tr><td>10 minutes
▪ Randy distributes the meeting notes to everyone before the Web Conference concludes.
▪ Bea gets a commitment for the next virtual meeting.
▪ Concluding remarks.</td></tr>
</table>

2-3: Expense Controls

Problem: The department was having difficulty staying within its budget. Many key team members were not at HQ.

Opportunity: Use Web Conferencing to increase awareness to the problem and to get commitment to remedies.

Frequency: Once or twice, or more frequently.

Participants: 15 people who know each other.

Behavioral: Information dissemination, light collaborative discussion, brainstorming, and agreed-on actions.

1½ hours – Content and Process
5 minutes ▪ Department head kicks off meeting and confirms everyone can "see" and "hear." Brief socialization.
25 minutes ▪ Department budget officer shows a variety of financial spreadsheets and reports: planned versus actual expense, vendor memos, and forecasts. Light discussion.
Break – 10 minutes
40 minutes ▪ Department head facilitates a brainstorming session. ▪ Ideas that are verbalized are typed so that everyone sees these ideas at the same time. ▪ Department head facilitates a collaborative discussion that leads to consensus on new processes, expense controls, and when to report financial variations. Discussion points are typed so everyone sees them.
10 minutes ▪ Wrap up and Next Steps. ▪ Discussion points are distributed to each participant.

2-4: Mentoring (Coaching)

Problem: The individuals in different cities had become frustrated with their "telephone only" mentoring sessions.

Opportunity: Use Web Conferencing to improve effectiveness. While talking, they want to "see" documents (project plans, status reports, and performance reviews) and to type into them.

Frequency: Monthly.

Participants: 2 people who know each other.

Behavioral: Collaborative discussion.

30 minutes – Content and Process
5 minutes ▪ Mentor (coach) confirms that the other person can "see" and "hear." ▪ They catch-up with each other – business and personal.
20 minutes ▪ Mentor (coach) opens the project plan which is seen by both parties. ▪ Mentor asks questions and listens to responses. ▪ Together, they discuss issues and solutions. ▪ Mentor types changes into the project plan. OR ▪ Person being mentored (coached) opens up documents on his or her PC and shows them to the mentor or coach. ▪ Types changes as appropriate.
5 minutes ▪ Debrief of this session. ▪ Homework assignment is agreed on.

2-5: Disaster Preparedness

Problem: The dispersed team had a history of conducting ineffective teleconferencing meetings.

Opportunity: The executive sponsor of disaster preparedness asks HR to assign an Organizational Development professional to facilitate virtual meetings using Web Conferencing. A key output is the revision of the real-life emergency preparedness drills.

Frequency: Ongoing meetings, before and after the actual emergency preparedness drills.

Participants: Global and Local IT, Human Resources, Facilities Management, Telecommuting Manager, and Organizational Development consultant.

Behavioral: These ongoing meetings have a good amount of collaborative discussion. Participants see and discuss different content (text documents, presentation slides, and project plans).

1 day – Content and Process
15 minutes ▪ Web Conferencing (WC) Leader confirms that everyone can "see" and "hear."

30 minutes
▪ Introductions are made, especially of new participants.
▪ Everyone sees and discusses the Agenda (text format).
▪ Optional:
  ▸ Chit-chat and catch up with each other.
  ▸ Show digitized pictures of participants in order to "socialize" the meeting.

continue to next page

2-5: Disaster Preparedness, *continued*

90 minutes
▪ One of the staff members keeps notes. ▪ Everyone sees a slide presentation that shows the major activities of the last emergency preparedness drill. ▪ Web Conferencing Leader shows and navigates through new Geographic Information System (GIS). Asks if it can be used to help store recruitment. ▪ Robust discussion: what worked well, problems, and improvement areas.
Break - 15 minutes
60 minutes
▪ Everyone sees the notes, which are in text format. ▪ Web Conferencing Leader facilitates discussion. ▪ A priority list of problems and improvement areas is written.
Break - 1 hour
75 minutes
▪ Web Conferencing Leader facilitates robust collaborative discussion on the priority list of problems and improvement areas. ▪ Outcome: specific actions for each. ▪ Project plan is updated – everyone sees this at the same time.
40 minutes
▪ Wrap up and Next Steps.

After the Web Conference
▪ Content from the meeting is made available on the intranet or team online workspace for the regular team members. It is e-mailed to the new people in attendance.

2-6: Employee Benefits – Large Audience

Problem: Employees throughout the enterprise were griping about not knowing much about the employee benefits.

Opportunity: Use Web Conferencing to get the message out with a degree of "real time" interactivity and Q&A.

Frequency: Periodic and as needed.

Participants: HR Benefits Managers, Group Benefits Consultant, Employees, and HR Coordinators in Regional and Local Offices. 10 – 2000 people at a time.

Behavioral: These Web Conferences vary in how they are delivered. *Here are several examples*:

- Web Conferences with HR Benefits Managers in regional and local offices. These virtual meetings are smaller in size and allow for more interactivity.

- Web Conferences with employees in regional and local offices. One HQ Benefits Manager can deliver information and respond to questions to multiple locations at the same time. Refer to the location examples in chapter one.

Web Conferencing can also be used for benefits communications between:

- HR and Finance
- HR and Labor Union
- HR and Benefits Consultants

Use Web Conferencing for New Initiatives

Use Web Conferencing virtual meetings to help you with these initiatives:

- ❑ Leadership Development
- ❑ Talent Management and Succession Planning
- ❑ Executive Education
- ❑ Blending delivery systems: eLearning and Synchronous Virtual Classroom
- ❑ Business Acumen Education for all employees
- ❑ LMS, LCMS, and HR Management Software
- ❑ Employee Involvement in Call Centers
- ❑ Performance Management System
- ❑ Virtual Working Skills
- ❑ Recruitment and On-Boarding
- ❑ Performance Appraisal
- ❑ Focus on the Customer
- ❑ ERP, CRM, M&A
- ❑ Business Restructuring
- ❑ Employee Retention Program
- ❑ HR Portal for Employees
- ❑ Mentored Learning
- ❑ PMO Portfolio Management
- ❑ Safety and Security
- ❑ Telecommuting

2-7: Project Kick-Offs

Problem: It was difficult to get key people to attend project kick-offs because of travel issues.

Opportunity: Use Web Conferencing for project kick-off meetings, so that everyone is on the same page from day one.

Frequency: At the beginning of new projects.

Participants: Project team members, project team manager, executive sponsor, and so forth.

Behavioral: The kick-off sessions start with introductions, followed by a formal lecture type presentation, followed by a highly interactive session.

1 - 3 hours – Content and Process
Before the Web Conference Starts ▪ Web Conferencing Technical Support ensures everything is working.

15 – 70 minutes ▪ Project Manager (PM) opens the Web Conference, welcomes everyone, and facilitates the initial introductions. ▪ Executive Sponsor and PM give a slide presentation, asking for participants to hold their questions.
Break – 10 minutes
30 – 70 minutes ▪ Executive Sponsor and PM open the meeting to questions. ▪ As questions are asked, they are typed so that all the participants see the questions. ▪ Executive Sponsor and Project Manager show additional content, which everyone sees at the same time.
5 - 30 minutes ▪ Debrief and Next Steps

2-8: Project Management

Problem: Most project team members worked in different locations. Project status meetings were ineffective because of distance problems.

Opportunity: Project Manager decides to use Web Conferencing to help everyone understand the responsibilities given to each person on the team.

Frequency: Weekly or bi-weekly.

Participants: Project team members (intact and new).

Behavioral: Expectation is to have a healthy amount of interplay among the team members. Larger issues that surface are assigned to a sub-group, so they can be reported on at next meeting.

1 hour – Content and Process
10 minutes ▪ It's Bill's turn to kick-off the meeting and to take notes on each person's hot issues. He types into a Hot Issues List (text document), which is seen by everyone.
30 minutes ▪ Project manager now takes the lead and shows the project plan (project management software) to everyone. As participants give their updates, he types into the project plan, which is seen by everyone.
15 minutes ▪ Several team members show their work in progress (deliverables – text documents, presentations, digitized photographs, financial spreadsheets, and so forth). ▪ Jane demonstrates navigation of the new web portal.
During the Web Conference ▪ Bill sends Hot Issues List to participants.
5 minutes ▪ Wrap up. *"Keep Up The Great Work !"*

2-9: Performance Management

Problem: The extended team had people in many different locations. It was tasked with revamping the company's performance management program. There were definite distance problems facing this team.

Opportunity: Use Web Conferencing to ensure robust communication for brainstorming, document reviews, and decision-making.

Frequency: Web Conferences over a five month period.

Participants: 14 people, some are new to each other.

Behavioral: It varies depending on the type of meeting. Socialization, analyze information, generating ideas, collaborative discussion, and decision-making.

1 ½ hours – Content and Process Force Field Analysis
15 minutes ▪ Web Conferencing Leader confirms everyone can "see" and "hear."
70 minutes ▪ Project Lead conducts a "Force Field Analysis" for the Performance Management system. A 2 column text document is opened and shown to everyone. ➢ In the left column, the project lead types in the "*Restraining Forces*" as they are discussed by the participants. ➢ In the right column, the project lead types in the "*Driving Forces*" as they are discussed.
5 minutes ▪ The participants schedule another Web Conference because they need more time.

2-10: HR Portal

Problem: The web portal was to go through a major refresh. The previous refresh resulted in costly rework and user complaints.

Opportunity: Use Web Conferencing to ensure project success. This includes tighter project management, virtual focus groups, enhanced coordination among developers in dispersed locations, and large audience sessions to promote the new site.

Frequency: As needed, before final decisions are made.

Participants: Software and web developers, stakeholders, Chief Learning Officer, Human Resources Executive, and users (executives, managers, and employees of the portal).

Behavioral: The Web Conferences allow "users" to give verbal feedback on what they see presented to them. The Web Conferences also allow the users to work in the portal so that the software and web development team can observe keystrokes and navigation being made by the users.

1 ¼ hours – Content and Process
15 minutes ▪ Person who initiated the Web Conference confirms that everyone can "see" and "hear." ▪ Project lead reviews the memo which had been sent out ahead of time. Expectations are agreed to.
45 minutes ▪ Mac shows and reviews requirements documents. ▪ Mac shows and navigates around the web portal. ▪ Users give verbal feedback. ▪ Developers see users navigating around into the portal.
15 minutes ▪ Wrap up and Next Steps.

2-11: Requirements

Problem: Too many projects and initiatives were suffering from changing requirements. This caused delays and costly change orders with vendors. (Sometimes the projects are implemented "on time," yet few users were satisfied.)

Opportunity: Use Web Conferencing as a tool to get at a better understanding of requirements.

Frequency: As needed.

Participants: Internal customers (in different locations), business process analysts, technical people, SMEs, vendors, software developers, sponsor, champion, and so forth.

Here are a few examples of different ways to use Web Conferencing when gathering requirements.

IF	THEN
If no requirements have been documented,	one of the participants types information that everyone sees at the same time.
If some requirements have been documented,	show what has been completed to the participants. During discussion, type changes and ideas that you hear.
If preliminary work has been completed on software screens or web pages,	show the screens and pages. Type information into the fields and/or show the page navigation. Take notes on what the users tell you.

2-12: Enterprise Resource Planning

Problem: The initiative was an ERP for a multi-location organization. The senior leadership team recognized there was too much silo thinking in the organization. Also, similar projects suffered from poor communications. The project sponsor contacted the Organizational Development (OD) staff to help in planning and implementing the ERP integration.

Opportunity: Use Web Conferencing with skilled facilitators, to conduct virtual meetings. The overall goal is to get the process correct and have wonderful results.

Frequency: Ongoing meetings to plan the change process and after the integration's kick off.

Participants: It varies. Some Web Conferences have new people attending, whereas others are with an intact work team.

Here are a few ideas for using Web Conferencing:

Employee Involvement	Virtual focus groups to learn first-hand about organizational barriers to success of the project.
Business Impacts and Business Processes	Cross-functional and multi-location meetings so that participants can discuss how their work impacts other areas.
Program Management	Virtual meetings with project managers.
Project Management	Virtual team meetings.
Change Management	Virtual meetings to develop the change management component.
Education and Training	Virtual sessions so that "everyone" hears the same thing at the same time.

2-13: Post Mortems (After Action Reviews)

Problem: The department head and project lead wanted to ensure an interactive discussion among the dispersed team and to document the lessons learned. There was no money for travel. They felt that e-mail did not get at the deeper lessons.

Opportunity: Use Web Conferencing to brainstorm on lessons learned, e.g. *what worked* and *what did not work.*

Frequency: At the end of a project, or at the end of a large milestone of a project.

Participants: Team members, sponsor, and client (optional).

Behavioral: High involvement with each person having a chance to contribute. Set the ground rule of focusing on learning, listening, and not fixing the blame or punishing anyone. Plan ahead with your questions, so that you get people talking to each other.

1 hour – Content and Process
5 minutes ▪ Web Conferencing Meeting Leader kicks off meeting and confirms everyone can see and hear.
45 minutes ▪ Leader announces objectives and ground rules. ▪ Everyone commits to the objectives and ground rules. ▪ Leader shows one or two slides, containing the project vision, objectives, and accomplishments. ▪ A team member volunteers to take notes while people are speaking – notes that everyone can see at the same time. ▪ As participants give their input, it is written so everyone can see it.
10 minutes ▪ Wrap up. ▪ Next steps are identified. (Optional)

Use Web Conferencing for Managing Relationships

Use Web Conferencing virtual meetings to help you with these activities:

- ❑ Being in the loop with stakeholders. *Are your resources aligned to the needs of the business?*
- ❑ Providing virtual OD services - facilitating a virtual meeting to help your client diagnose a performance problem.
- ❑ Listening to your client's business strategy, objectives, plans, and obstacles.
- ❑ Managing an outsourcer's service contract or monthly performance report.
- ❑ Collaborating on a proposed statement of work that your department is to provide.
- ❑ Facilitating a meeting where you and your client collaboratively arrive at a solution to a problem.
- ❑ Training your client's staff how to complete a new performance appraisal system.
- ❑ Discussing, collaborating, and getting commitment to your recommendations.
- ❑ Coordinating a roll-out schedule with your internal client.
- ❑ Discussing information that resides in an application, such as LMS or HR Information System.
- ❑ Surfing the Internet together to spot appropriate conference facilities.

2-14: Outsourcing

Problem: Management was concerned with the outsourcing relationship. They felt it had eroded, more from neglect than from anything else. Dispersed locations made it very difficult to have face-to-face meetings with all the people who needed to attend.

Opportunity: Use Web Conferencing for monthly virtual meetings to ensure better management and cost controls.

Frequency: Monthly and as needed.

Participants: 6-10 people, from the company and the outsourcer.

Behavioral: Discussions to enhance communication, coordination, and management processes.

80 minutes – Content and Process
10 minutes ▪ Web Conferencing Leader (person who called the Web Conference) confirms that all the participants can "see" and "hear."
50 minutes ▪ Review of agenda (which had been sent out beforehand). ▪ Additional agenda items are asked for and added. ▪ Relationship Manager opens the Open Items Report and goes through each and every item. ▪ Status is discussed and agreed upon, then typed into the report so that everyone sees it at the same time. ▪ Open discussion about the business relationship.
20 minutes ▪ Debrief and Next Steps. ▪ Open Items Report is emailed to all participants.

2-15: Enterprise Learning Council

Problem: Many of the scheduled monthly meetings of the Enterprise Learning Council were cancelled. Too many people did not want to travel to attend.

Opportunity: Use Web Conferencing for the monthly meetings.

Frequency: Monthly.

Participants: 10 – 25 people. Inter-disciplinary membership, representing line departments, business development, executives, suppliers and partners, IT, and sometimes outside speakers.

Behavioral: Presentations and light discussions. Sometimes they dig into critical issues.

Here are a few ideas for using Web Conferencing:

eLearning	Virtual brainstorming on issues to be faced in 2-3 years.
Innovation	Show a condensed version of innovation report. Discussion on next steps. Document the discussion.
Health Promotion	Make decision on expansion of the program or maintain "as is."
Web 2.0	Remote presentations by leading consultants. Brainstorm on this trend. Discussion on next steps. Document the discussion during the Web Conference.
Leadership	Virtual sessions on the subject of: *What leadership traits will we need in 2-5 years?*

2-16: Organizational Development

Problem: Last year there was a huge budget for the call center initiative. It included travel and lodging for change agents. However, after the rollout there was not a travel budget for the change agents. The Call Centers still needed organizational development support. There was a serious concern about backsliding to the old ways.

Opportunity: Organizational Development (OD) consultants and trainers use Web Conferencing to provide virtual interventions and support.

Frequency: Monthly and as needed.

Participants: 2-100 people, including OD consultants.

Behavioral: Training follow-up, coaching, brainstorming, discussions, and problem diagnosis.

Here are a few ideas for using Web Conferencing:

People are reverting to past (old) behaviors	Virtual sessions to discuss management options and possible interventions.
Cycle times between groups is declining, not improving	Show the flow charts and diagnose where the blockages are. Get commitment to make required changes.
Management reports are under-utilized	Show reports. Share examples on using these by Center Managers and First-Line Supervisors.
Absenteeism	Brainstorm on reducing this problem.

2-17: University Partnership

Problem: There was a desire to reduce how much time was spent traveling to a central location for monthly meetings.

Opportunity: Use Web Conferencing for synchronous virtual meetings.

Frequency: Each quarter, two Web Conferences and one face-to-face meeting.

Participants: University and Company leaders and managers.

Behavioral: These Web Conferences are collegial in style, usually with presentations and discussions.

3 hours – Content and Process
15 minutes ▪ Rob kicks off the meeting and confirms that everyone can "see" and "hear." ▪ Participants show images of their family.
150 minutes ▪ Rob shows several presentation slides that describes the partnership's vision and goals. ▪ In this virtual meeting, they want to compare their partnership's web site with those from other universities. ▪ Rob navigates through these web sites. ▪ Luis facilitates a discussion of what they viewed. ▪ During this discussion, Samantha keeps notes that everyone sees at the same time.
15 minutes ▪ Rob asks for several participants to provide a summary and suggestions for possible next steps. ▪ Wrap up and Next Steps.

2-18: Local Schools Partnership

Problem: The school district had tremendous need for subject experts to give classroom talks and for more youth tutors. Developing an approach had been put off because of distance problems. In addition, there were questions about using synchronous Web Conferencing for some of the talks and tutoring.

Opportunity: Web Conferencing is used by the staffs to formulate a proposal for using Web Conferencing for virtual classroom teaching and for youth mentoring. During these virtual sessions, the staffs are also able to gauge when best to use Web Conferencing with the youth.

Frequency: Weekly.

Participants: 2 – 10 people.

Behavioral: Highly interactive.

1 hour – Content and Process
5 minutes ▪ Person who started the Web Conference confirms that the other participants can "see" and "hear."
45 minutes ▪ The participants co-create text documents and presentations that support this proposed innovative program. Their document is to contain the problem statement, goals, obstacles, benefits, technology, outcomes, training, selection criteria, sponsorship, startup and recurring costs, and grants.
10 minutes ▪ During the Web Conference, the written documents are distributed to each participant. ▪ Wrap-up. Set date and time for next Web Conference.

Use Web Conferencing for Learning and Training

The following categories are the steps in the A.D.D.I.E. Instructional Systems Design (ISD) model.

Analysis

- ☐ Involving front-line people in the field to identify and verify training gaps and organizational culture issues that impact performance. (Virtual Needs Assessment)
- ☐ Involving stakeholders and field managers to understand their visions and perception of performance problems.

Design

- ☐ Collaboratively discuss interactive teaching techniques and delivery options for specific courses and audiences.
- ☐ Brainstorming and building consensus for a blended learning design. Participants include classroom instructors, elearning developers, leader-led virtual instructors (synchronous), and mobility technologists.

Development

- ☐ Project status sessions for discussing development schedules, milestones, and content review dates.
- ☐ Co-creation among SMEs and colleagues.
- ☐ Walk-through of materials.

Implementation (Delivery)

- ☐ Facilitating, and co-facilitating, high quality, interactive, interesting distance learning (virtual learning) classes.
- ☐ Leading large audience knowledge classes for hundreds of people at a time. (Instructor in a separate location.)

Evaluation

- ☐ Collaboratively reach a decision on how to best administer a Level 3 Evaluation (transfer of learning to the workplace after the training).

When Web Conferencing is used for distance learning, it is often referred to as a *Virtual Instructor-Led Classroom, Instructor-Led Real-Time Online Training, or Synchronous Virtual Classroom.*

Distance Learning

"Distance education is a planned teaching/learning experience that uses a wide spectrum of technologies to reach learners at a distance and is designed to encourage learner interaction and certification of learning."

Used with permission of:
Instructional Communications Systems at the University of Wisconsin-Extension. http://www.uwex.edu/ics/design/webcon.htm
Copyright, 2006. Board of Regents. University of Wisconsin

Blended Learning

"Blended learning is the combination of multiple approaches to pedagogy or teaching." From Wikipedia, the free encyclopedia

***

"In general I would agree with the above definition, where "approaches" is understood to mean instructional media, such as instructor-led training (ILT), self-paced e-learning modules, readings, etc. The advent of robust online synchronous and asynchronous collaboration tools has given new impetus to the blended learning movement, enabling organizations to reinforce one-time ILT or e-learning with web-based coached assignments, small group meetings, mentoring, and action plans; shifting the balance of "seat time" from the training event to post-training application and reinforcement."

Used with permission of: Bill Bruck, Ph.D. Principal, Q2Learning, LLC

2-19: Needs Assessment

Problem: The department head wanted the staff to involve more people in needs assessment, but not to sacrifice interactivity and "people touch." Many of these people were in multiple locations and there was no travel budget.

Opportunity: Web Conferencing is used to conduct virtual needs assessment meetings, with people at their own PC as well as people coming into a meeting room.

Frequency: At the beginning of new programs and projects.

Participants: Professional staff, consultants, and people in field and home offices.

Behavioral: Highly interactive.

Here are several ways to accomplish this.

1	**1:1's**. In this scenario, the Web Conferences are private. Content is shown. Questions are verbalized by the professional. Responses are recorded in real-time; both individuals see the responses.
2	**One staff (or consultant) and multiple people at their own PC**. This is similar to the above scenario, but 2-5 people are responding to the content shown and the questions.
3	**Meeting Rooms**. In this scenario, the people are in a meeting room (or rooms) and the staff person or consultant is remote. Content is shown and questions are responded to.

2-20: Blended Learning Strategy

Problem: The learning and training department was developing its Blended Learning strategy. They were not having the proper discussions with the dispersed team members.

Opportunity: Web Conferencing is used to help the team members clarify the goals and begin the process of program development.

Frequency: Weekly for several months.

Participants: Learning and training staff at HQ and in the field, consultants, internal customers, executives, employees, vendors, and consultants.

Behavioral: Depending on the agenda, Web Conferences range from information being presented to increase awareness and understanding with light Q&A, to highly interactive sessions.

Here are several examples of virtual meetings to get their arms around this topic.

1	During this Web Conference, participants see and listen to a virtual workshop on Blended Learning in the Workplace. This gets everyone oriented to possibilities.
2	During this Web Conference, the CLO gives a presentation on the impact to the business, if Blended Learning is used.
3	This Web Conference is designed so that the learning and training staff get input from their internal customers. The training manager shows a chart that identifies courses under consideration. Then, the learning and training staff listens and records what is said so everyone can see it at the same time.

2-21: Coaches Program

Problem: The requirements for the new front-line employee training program included a follow-up program that front-line coaches would implement after the front-line employees completed their classroom instruction. There were significant issues around time, timing, and processes that had to be worked out for the coaching interventions. Most of the front-line coaches and stakeholders worked in separate locations.

Opportunity: Web Conferencing is used to help the dispersed stakeholders and front-line coaches understand the issues, develop a successful program, and get buy-in by everyone.

Frequency: Several meetings a week until the issues are settled and documented.

Participants: Managers of first-line supervisors, first-line supervisors, training staff, and training consultant.

Behavioral: Participants look at and discuss weekly production charts, business process flow charts (current processes), staffing levels, and time cycles. There is consensus- building around short-term and long-term actionable recommendations.

continue to next page

2-21: Coaches Program, *continued*

2 hours – Content and Flow First Session – Entire Team
15 minutes ▪ Training manager confirms that everyone can "see" and "hear." ▪ Training consultant is tasked with keeping notes.
15 minutes ▪ Introductions are made. ▪ Training manager shows presentation to kick-off the meeting. Leads engaging discussion about why the coaches program is necessary.
70 minutes ▪ Training manager and one of the field coaches show the curriculum outline, proposed time frames, and the coach responsibilities. Everyone sees this at the same time. ▪ Training manager facilitates robust discussion, to identify problems with implementation. ▪ All notes are sent to participants.
20 minutes ▪ Wrap up and Next Steps.

2-22: Course Learning Objectives

Problem: With people in many different locations, it was difficult to get adequate discussion and consensus on course learning objectives. (In the past, the learning objectives were grandiose. In actuality, there was a big gap between the learning objectives and the actual training program.)

Opportunity: Web Conferencing is used to help spark candid communication and better clarification of the performance gaps and course's objectives.

Frequency: One or two meetings.

Participants: Training manager, Instructional Systems Designer, Target Audience Champion, and Consultant.

Behavioral: The participants see "draft" materials and they discuss and co-edit and co-create at the same time.

1 hour – Content and Process
5 minutes ▪ Web Conferencing Meeting Leader kicks off meeting and confirms everyone can see and hear.
45 minutes ▪ Web Conferencing Meeting Leader shows Learning Objectives (text document). ▪ As participants give their input, and the input is agreed to by everyone, the document is immediately edited so everyone can see it at the same time.
10 minutes ▪ Meeting Leader leads discussion on next steps. ▪ Revised learning objectives document is distributed or uploaded to a common location.

2-23: Course Content Development

Problem: The department had just one senior level course developer along with many inexperienced developers. All these people worked in separate offices or at home. The problem was the slow and less-than-high-quality of the new courses in development.

Opportunity: Use Web Conferencing to brainstorm, critique, and collaborate on course content development.

Frequency: As needed.

Participants: Senior level developer and junior developers.

Behavioral: These virtual meetings are meant to cover a lot of ground quickly. The participants see "draft" materials (storyboards and other) and they rapidly go through a collaborative discussion. (The senior developer also uses Web Conference for small impromptu classes, to give lessons and coaching to these junior developers.)

1 - 2 hours – Content and Process
5 minutes ▪ Web Conferencing Meeting Leader kicks off meeting and confirms the other person can "see" and "hear."
50 – 110 minutes ▪ Developer or Web Conferencing Meeting Leader shows materials to the other. ▪ Together, they quickly go from page to page to discuss the materials. ▪ The junior developer takes personal notes to use later on.
5 minutes ▪ Wrap up and Next Steps.

2-24: Client Reviews

Problem: The client was always late in reviewing e-mailed materials. This created severe time and sourcing issues, including extra shipping charges for materials that had to be express shipped to field locations.

Opportunity: Use Web Conferencing for "walk throughs" of your draft (or "near final") deliverables. Get faster sign-offs.

Frequency: As needed.

Participants: People in the client environment, plus learning and training staff. At times, you may want to include the Project Sponsor for part of the virtual meeting.

Behavioral: These meetings are meant to review and get consensus on the draft deliverables. The participants see and discuss "draft" materials. In some meetings, there might be radical changes, whereas in most meetings, the approach is to fine-tune what has already been created.

1 - 2 hours – Content and Process
10 minutes ▪ Web Conferencing Meeting Leader kicks off meeting and confirms everyone can "see" and "hear."
30 – 90 minutes ▪ Web Conferencing Meeting Leader shows materials to everyone. ▪ Course developer leads the walk-through. ▪ Try to avoid getting bogged down. These subjects, when necessary, should be worked on later on. ▪ As the client representatives give their input, and when there is agreement, the changes are made immediately in the documents, or they are made afterwards.
20 minutes ▪ Wrap up and Next Steps.

2-25: Follow-Up Training Class

Problem: Although most of the people completed the self-paced course, a significant number of people still had questions on several critical parts of the curriculum.

Opportunity: The used Web Conferencing. The SME, located in one of the regions, answered the questions of the dispersed people.

Frequency: Within two weeks of the completed self-paced course, and as needed.

Participants: Participation is voluntary, except when the supervisor mandates it.

Behavioral: Participants see visual representations of the self-paced course, with opportunity for explanation and Q&A.

1 hour – Content and Process
Before the Web Conference ▪ Questions are emailed to the SME.

10 minutes ▪ SME confirms that everyone can "see" and "hear." ▪ SME uses a polling tool to query the participants.
40 minutes ▪ SME shows visuals from the self-paced course. (In most cases, there is no need to take time to create anything new.) ▪ SME gives explanations, asks questions, and responds to questions, all with the objective of overcoming confusion and to provide clarification.
10 minutes ▪ How to submit additional questions. ▪ Wrap up.

2-26: Advanced Train-The-Trainer

Problem: Typically, the Instructors came to a central location for several days of Train-The-Trainer. There was no follow-up training and this had a negative impact on course delivery.

Opportunity: Use Web Conferencing to make the Train-The-Trainer more of a process of learning. Rather than a one-time event, use the virtual classroom to provide additional content to those who desire it.

Frequency: Ongoing, every week for two months.

Participants: Training delivery staff and consultants who had completed the Train-The-Trainer program.

Behavioral: A curriculum for the two month period is used so that the sessions did not get stale. Trainers present and/or give solutions to scenarios that are provided. There is expert feedback and peer discussion.

30 - 60 Minutes – Content and Process
5 minutes ▪ Master Trainer confirms that everyone can "see" and "hear." ▪ Agenda is discussed. Additional items are added or put in the parking lot.
20 – 50 minutes ▪ Trainers show parts of a module, give a demo, and get feedback. ▪ The SME joins the Web Conference and shows additional content and answers questions. ▪ Classroom management issues are discussed, along with solutions. ▪ Ideation on how to get higher quality involvement by the supervisors of the classroom participants.
5 minutes ▪ Wrap up.

2-27: Software/Systems Learning

Problem: A key component of the organizational transformation project was to make major changes to an existing computer system. This system was used by 5 people in each of the 15 field offices. Changes had been made, but there was no budget to get people together and the documentation was inadequate.

Opportunity: Two SMEs in different locations use Web Conferencing to train the users in the other locations.

Frequency: Three days a week for a number of weeks.

Participants: Participation is voluntary.

Behavioral: Virtual classes are informal. Most of the participants knew each other. Participants see and discuss system screens.

1 hour – Content and Process
5 minutes ▪ Field expert confirms that everyone can "see" and "hear."
50 minutes ▪ SME (field expert) shows and discusses the new screens, navigation, data entry, reports, and work-arounds.
5 minutes ▪ Wrap up.

2-28: Evaluation

Problem: The dispersed team was at the beginning steps in developing (or revising) their learning and training evaluation process.

Opportunity: Use Web Conferencing for the dispersed team and for sub-groups within the team.

Frequency: Once a week for several months.

Participants: HQ and Field learning and training staff, plus supervisors and managers who have expressed interest.

Behavioral: The early virtual meetings are informal. Most of the participants know each other. Participants discuss the content they see at the same time.

1 hour – Content and Process
5 minutes ▪ Meeting leader asks if everyone can "see" and "hear."
50 minutes ▪ Meeting leader opens her Internet browser and does a search on "Kirkpatrick Evaluation." ▪ Meeting leader shows this web content. It is used as a jumping off point for ideas and discussion. ▪ Throughout the discussion, the meeting leader keeps notes that everyone sees at the same time.
5 minutes ▪ Wrap up and Next Steps.

Blended Learning Examples

In this chapter, I present different ways to engage the *employees* (*students*, learners, *adult learners*, *trainees, participants*).

These examples, however, do not emphasize detailed instructional strategies, specific content, "how much" and "how often" is needed.

I do subscribe to these three components (activities) in the learning and development process.

- ***Learning** a subject and/or task (Knowledge and Skill Acquisition)*
- ***Application** (Apply the Knowledge / Skill)*
- ***Expert Feedback** (and/or Expert Modeling)*

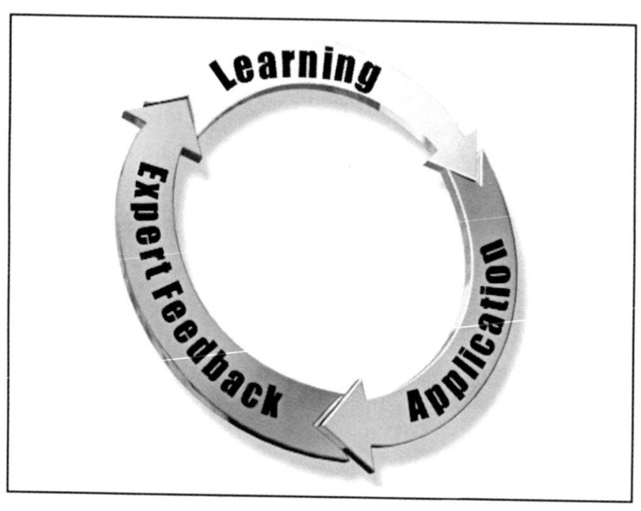

2-29: Two Day Learning Program

Problem: For budget reasons, the organization needed to convert a two day (13 hours of instruction) instructor-led live classroom training course into a "*blended learning*" format.

Opportunity: Use Web Conferencing for course delivery of a major portion of the learning.

Frequency: See schedule below.

Participants: Participation is mandatory.

Behavioral: This chart shows the blended learning design. The total instructional time is more than fifteen hours.

Learning Tasks		Minutes
Module 1:	Participants must complete a self-paced, pre-course assignment.	90
Module 2:	Participants submit a completed quiz, based on the self-paced assignment.	15
Module 3:	First Virtual Classroom. Includes Web Conferencing practice time. The *next page has details.*	180
Module 4:	Participants pair up and complete an assignment before the next class.	30
Module 5:	Second Virtual Classroom.	150
Module 6:	Participants pair up and complete an assignment. Feedback from local SMEs.	90
Module 7:	Third Virtual Classroom.	150
Module 8:	Participants work alone to complete an assignment.	30
Module 9:	Fourth Virtual Classroom.	150
Module 10:	Participants complete a test.	60

2-29: Two Day Learning Program,

continued

Module 3 Example 3 hours – Content and Process
45 minutes ▪ Virtual Instructor confirms that everyone can "see" and hear." ▪ Instructor explains the Web Conferencing interactive tools and participants have time to practice them. ▪ Virtual Instructor presents course learning objectives. ▪ Participants give reasons why they are attending and what they want to achieve in the course. These are written for everyone to see.
60 minutes ▪ Virtual Instructor debriefs the pre-course assignment. ▪ Participants respond to Polling / Survey questions. ▪ Instructor gives presentation. ▪ Discussion and Q&A.
Break - 15 minutes
45 minutes ▪ Two participants read the case study. ▪ Virtual Instructor facilitates a high-involvement, robust discussion about the case study. Input from all the participants is sought. ▪ Comments and ideas are written so that everyone can see them.
15 minutes ▪ Virtual Instructor explains the assignment. ▪ Module 3 wrap-up.

2-30: Blended Learning Process (A)

Employees (students, adult learners) read a 5-page document, sent via e-mail or retrieved from their Learning Content Management System (LCMS).

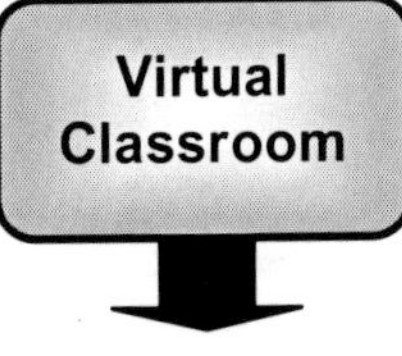

3 days later, students participate in a Virtual Instructor-Led Classroom (Web Conference) session.

Next day, local managers engage students to verify learning and to coach.

2-31: Blended Learning Process (B)

Students view and listen to a movie clip, sent via e-mail or retrieved from a Learning Content Management System (LCMS).

2 days later, students participate in a Virtual Instructor-Led Classroom.

Students complete an on-the-job activity.

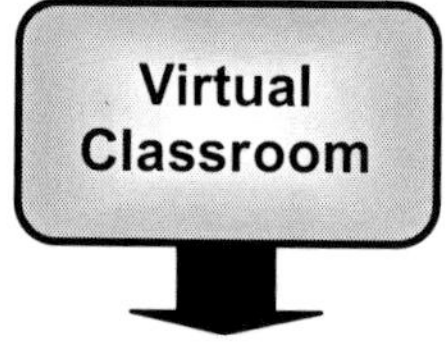

3 days later, students participate in a Virtual Leader-Led Classroom and work in small teams.

Students complete another on-the-job activity.

Local supervisors give feedback on the activity.

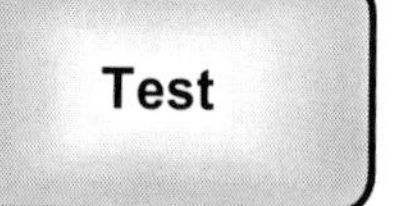

Students complete a test. If they pass, they are able to proceed to the next chunk of learning and mastery.

2-32: Blended Learning Process (C)

Learners listen to audio clips they downloaded from the company's intranet.

Learners complete a self-paced learning module. (Retrieved from their organization's intranet, LMS (Learning Management System), or LCMS (Learning Content Management System).

During the following week, they attend a Virtual Instructor-Led Classroom.

Learners exchange information with each other and a virtual SME (subject matter expert), using an "Asynchronous" Online Virtual Team Workroom.

The virtual SME posts feedback in the "Asynchronous" Online Virtual Team Workroom.

2-33: Blended Learning Process (D)

Employees in multiple regions are given case study assignments to read and analyze.

For the next three weeks, the employees work in small teams and use Web Conferencing to discuss and create their solution to the case study.

After the case study solutions are completed, Web Conferencing is used so that each team can report out to the other participants.

- Expert Feedback: Case study experts listen to and give feedback on each team's solution.

Within two weeks, each team is to write up and distribute their "Lessons Learned."

The case study experts co-facilitate a Virtual Instructor-Led Classroom experience for all the students.

- This session serves as an overall debriefing.

2-34: Blended Learning Process (E)

Learners attend a live, face-to-face leader-led class.

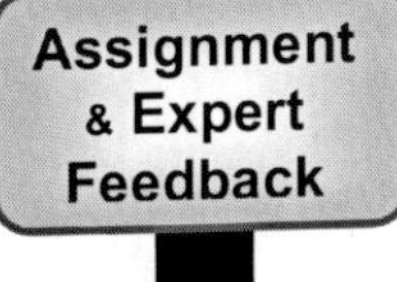

After the class, the learners complete an assignment, which is reviewed by their local manager or local mentor (coach). Learners are given feedback and/or get to see the mentor perform the task.

Virtual Classroom

A week later, the learners participate in a Virtual Instructor-Led Classroom.

2-35: Blended Learning Process (F)

Learners attend Live and Virtual Instructor-Led Classroom sessions to kick-off the Leadership, Technical, or Legal program.

Employees enter the campus with a user id and password. While in the virtual campus, they:

- Socialize and build relationships with other learners, in small and large groups.
- Understand assignments, see the overall program calendar, download content, and post questions.
- See what learning modules and activities they have completed or not completed.
- See dates / times for Synchronous Classroom sessions.
- Get feedback from virtual coaches and SMEs
- Complete group activities and mastery tests.
- Read and contribute to "blogs" and "wikis."
- Maintain a journal and complete mastery tests.

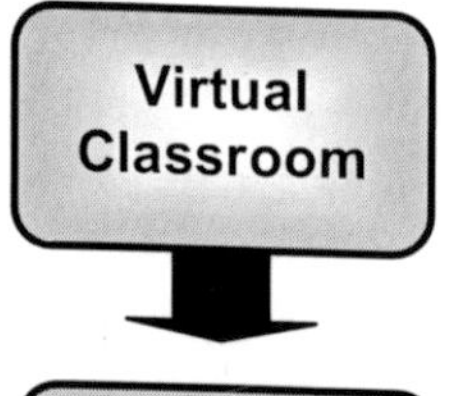

Learners interact with real-life customers, executives, and managers. Learners also collaborate together on case studies.

Virtual Experts give "real-time" feedback and coaching to the entire class and to learners grouped by knowledge / experience level.

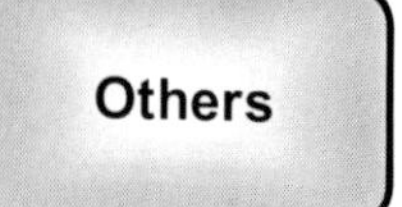

OTHERS WHO USE THE VIRTUAL ASYNCHRONOUS CAMPUS

- **Virtual Experts:** Post content in response to learner questions and the learners' completed assignments.
- **Administrators:** See learner completion rates and print reports.

Final Note

The Learning Mantra: Why are we here?

✓ Training/education is the process
✓ Learning is the outcome
✓ The technology is the means

The learner is why we are here!
Focus on learning outcomes...the end result:

Improving human performance

By permission of Dr. Jolly T. Holden
Dr. Jolly T. Holden is a learning consultant.
He is President Emeritus of the United States Distance Learning Association (USDLA).

Additional information about Blended Learning:

www.MoreVirtual.com

Free Stuff page – Blended Learning section

Notes

Chapter 3

Tips and Techniques

Chapter Objectives

After reading this chapter, you are able to:

- Describe, discuss, and apply tips and techniques for developing your Web Conferencing skills.
- Describe methods for optimizing Web Conferencing in organizations and agencies.
- Discuss how a Web Conferencing Product Manager could enhance the success of Web Conferencing in your organization.
- Describe the benefits of using a Web Conferencing Planning and Interface Group.

Tips and Techniques Content

Although most people can begin using Web Conferencing in fifteen minutes or less, these tips are offered to help a person expand his or her awareness and to develop one's skills.

This chapter contains sixty-five tips and techniques. They are organized into seven categories.

- Organizational Development
- Getting Started
- Planning and Preparing Your Web Conferences
- Building Relationships
- Engaging and Involving Participants
- Developing Your Web Conferencing Skills
- Extra Tips

A list of these tips and techniques, along with their page number, is contained in the next few pages.

Organizational Development

These tips and techniques are to help organizations optimize the use of Web Conferencing.

Tip #1. Develop a Web Conferencing Mindset

One of the ways to optimize Web Conferencing is for people to develop a Web Conferencing Mindset. Here are several questions you and your staff should be asking:

Do I really have to travel to this meeting?

How can we get that person's expertise into our team? (The person works in another building or hundreds/thousands of miles away.)

What can we do to improve collaboration, communication, coordination, consensus-building, and decision-making among team members who don't work under the same roof?

What opportunities are we missing because of the distance factor?

What telephone and conference calls would benefit by adding the "visual" component?

Tip #2. Appoint a Person to the Role of Web Conferencing Product Manager

Many organizations buy new software and solutions to achieve better communications and efficiencies. Yet, sometimes the "planned results" do not yet match the "actual results." To avoid this dilemma and to optimize the use of Web Conferencing, I suggest organizations appoint someone to serve the role of Web Conferencing Product Manager. The responsibilities and time involved are likely to fluctuate (1 hours a week? 20 hours a week?) depending on needs of the organization.

Responsibilities can include:

- **Market Size and Opportunities**: Conduct research with executives and line of business managers. Identify the market and opportunities.

- **Internal Promotion**: Develop and distribute promotional materials and track and communicate success stories.

- **Training and Evaluation**: Identify training needs, coordinate training delivery, and evaluate training. Participate with internal customers, technical resources and vendor(s) to assess usage and related issues.

- **Special Services**: Develop partnerships and alliances with special audiences or initiatives, such as:

  - Learning Organizations / Training Department
  - Workflow Process Management
  - Organizational Development
  - Human Resources - Employee Communications
  - Reorganization Leaders
  - Integration Champions and Sponsors

Tip #3. Identify and Align Resources

Web Conferencing software keeps getting better and better, with more and more useful features. That's the good news. But sometimes those wonderful features go underutilized because using them can be a bit daunting at first for a person who is new to Web Conferencing.

Recommendation: Identify resources that can be helpful to Web Conferencing users. Then, align these resources to teams and individuals. For example, multimedia talent can be helpful to Web Conference Leaders and Presenters.

Recommendation: Organize a Web Conferencing Planning and Interface Group that meets on a regular basis. Agenda items can include planning, coordination, and continuous improvement strategies. It is comprised of:

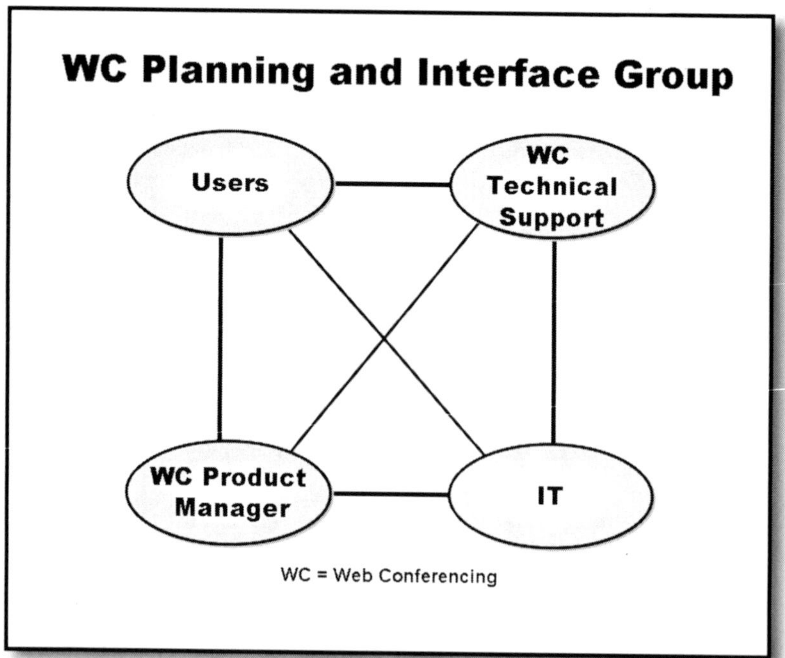

Tip #4. Identify Geographic Footprint (Physical Locations)

Analyze your organization's (department, function) geographical footprint. (Where are the facilities and people?)

Tip #5. Identify Workflow Processes

Identify organizational processes that could be modified and improved by using Web Conferencing.

Tip #6. Analyze Travel Budgets and Travel Patterns

Analyze travel budgets and determine the amount of expense that could be cut by using Web Conferencing. Where do you and others travel to meetings?

Tip #7. Setup a Web Conferencing Service Center

Staff a service center with virtual employees who can lend a hand to help Web Conferencing users at different sites. Web Conferencing users should be able to easily make requests and to receive assistance.

I need help with (check all that apply):

- ❑ Web Conference: 15 people at their own PC, inside our firewall, plus 10 people from outside our department
- ❑ Web Conference: 60+ people
- ❑ Some participants will use Windows XP and some MacOS
- ❑ Animation (to loop before the session formally starts
- ❑ Polls, Surveys, Tests (if these are available)
- ❑ Insert a MPEG movie into a presentation
- ❑ VoIP or Microphone
- ❑ Record a Web Conference session
- ❑ Very large session or using an outside service bureau
- ❑ LAN/Internet Access from specific meeting rooms
- ❑ Projector, Electronic Whiteboard, Electronic Pen, Headsets

Tip #8. Create Attention with Prizes and Mementos

When kicking off or expanding the use of Web Conferencing, consider giving out prizes for attendance and participation. (This might be especially important if your organization's culture gives out prizes and mementos for other types of kick-offs.)

Getting Started

These tips and techniques are important to people who are just beginning to think about using Web Conferencing.

Tip #9. Know Your Resources

When not familiar with the Web Conference medium, contact your Web Conference Leader or Web Conference Coordinator. They will help you understand what resources are available. Discuss what you plan to do during the Web Conference and ask if there are any special considerations. For example, do you have a slide presentation or financial spreadsheet on your computer that you want everyone to see? Do you need to forward your file(s) to the Web Conference Leader or Web Conference Coordinator before the scheduled date and time of the Web Conference?

Tip #10. Have Someone Else "Push" the Slides and Handle the Web Conferencing Interactions and Annotation Tools

There could be situations when you are brand-new to Web Conferencing and you are called upon to give a presentation, lead the session, or facilitate a group discussion. Find someone who can assist you by "pushing" the presentation slides and handling the interactive and markup tools. That person can literally be next to you, using your computer with you. Or, the person can be located hundreds or thousands of miles away.

Tip #11. Perform a System Check of Your Computer

As a new user and if people are connecting to a Web Conference from multiple locations, I encourage you to perform the system check before the Web Conference. Communicate with Web Conferencing Technical Support, if needed.

As a "Presenter," does your PC meet the system requirements (e.g. do you plan to use a webcam)? What are the system requirements for the "Participants"? Do they need Flash or a presentation software player on their PC?

Tip #12. Attend Web Conferences

If Web Conferencing is brand-new to you and if you are on tap to perform at an upcoming Web Conference session, attend one or two beforehand. Just remember, not all Web Conferences are alike. For example, a Web Conferencing used for a project team status is different than a highly collaborative session or a presentation.

Observe techniques and practices. Ask yourself, "*How can I optimize the use of Web Conferencing?* "*How can we use Web Conferencing in our organization?*

If you are not able to observe a Web Conference by sitting next to someone who is participating, get permission to log in to the sessions and observe from your computer.

Planning and Preparing Your Web Conferences

These tips and techniques are helpful as you plan and prepare your Web Conferences.

Tip #13. Set Objectives. Then, Match Content to the Objectives (Outcomes)

Make sure the content of the Web Conference matches its objectives. Identify carefully the exact content to be shown and discussed.

Tip #14. Match Web Conferencing "Design" to the Web Conferencing Objectives (Outcomes)

What "flow" or "process" should your Web Conference follow to in order to assure your objectives (outcomes) are achieved? What amount of involvement and interaction is important for your participants?

A WC (Web Conference) Designer may not be important for brief Web Conferences (like those held by an intact team, a person with "meeting design" or "meeting planning" experience).

However, a WC Designer could be very helpful for mid-size and very large Web Conferences.

Training and development professionals, with instructional design and/or training facilitation experience, are very good at offering excellent suggestions on ways to achieve interaction and engagement for participants.

You might want to design-in the use of **polls** or **surveys.** Or, your design could include dividing participants into **breakout teams**, where they work on a problem or assignment in small groups.

Tip #15. Create a "Virtual Roundtable" Experience

When you want your participants to hear at the same time from multiple experts (located in different cities), design your Web Conference so there is a roundtable discussion experience. Someone plays the role of moderator and the experts play off of each other, during the presentations, discussions, and/or the Q&A.

Tip #16. Use Multiple Speakers to Keep Things Interesting

Another technique for keeping the Web Conferencing interesting is to use multiple presenters on the same subject. If you are using presentation slides, one person can be responsible for the odd number slides and the other person for the even number slides, or some such method.

Tip #17. Know Your Audience – Prepare Yourself and Other Presenters and SMEs

Knowing your audience helps in prepping yourself, other Presenters and those in the role of a SME.

- **Motivation of participants**: Why are people attending? Is attendance mandatory? What's the WIIFM (What's In It For Me) factor for each person? Any hidden agendas?

- **Pre-Web Conference assignments**: Knowing your audience helps you determine whether or not to use Pre-Web Conference assignments. If you use a Pre-Web Conference assignment that only fifty per cent of the participants complete ahead of time, you could have problems during your Web Conference.

- **What phase is the group or team in?** One approach is a "Forming, Storming, Norming, and Performing" model. When planning a Web Conference for a small group or team, know what phase they are in. Having people at different phases could impact the group or team's behavior. Do a search at www.wikipedia.org; type in these words (forming, storming, norming, performing) for an interesting description.

- **Scouting report**: If you are a virtual facilitator for a group with whom you have little contact, it can be helpful to know something about the participants. For example, who is usually the quiet one during a meeting, who is known as the thinker, who tends to dominate a meeting, what are the reporting relationships, and so forth.

- **Plan ahead for challenging subjects and audiences**: For a difficult audience in a face-to-face meeting, you would plan ahead. Do the same with your Web Conferences. One technique is to touch base with one or two individuals prior to the Web Conference and discuss a strategy for handling a sensitive issue or how to design the session so people with opposing points of view can begin to come together.

Tip #18. Provide Assistance to Outside Speakers and SMEs

If you have an outside speaker or SME scheduled for a Web Conference, who may not be familiar with the Web Conferencing medium, contact this person a week before (or at least several days) before the conference. This allows you to support and address this person's needs.

Tip #19. Set Expectations, Then Follow Through with Them

The willingness to use and participate in Web Conferencing is often influenced by what people experience when they first begin attending Web Conferences. If you tell participants there is going to be a good amount of discussion, Q&A, and/or collaboration and yet you lead the Web Conference in a manner where you or someone else talks 95% of the time, you are getting off to a bad start.

It is important to set expectations upfront with participants. For example, if one objective is to have a lot of collaborative discussion, tell participants this is one of the meeting's objectives. Also tell/show which Web Conferencing tools you want them to use; e.g. hand raising, chat, checkmark annotations, or something else.

Real Life Example: Here's a real-life example of how a team using Web Conferencing for the first time, can get off to a bad start.

- The manager communicated to the team: We'll have a one hour Web Conference, with 30 minutes for a slide presentation and the remaining time for robust discussion with Q&A.

- The team experienced: The manager speaking for fifty-five minutes and taking questions for only five minutes.

Tip #20. Schedule Breaks

I encourage you to take breaks for lengthy Web Conferences. You can set the break time yourself and review it when you discuss the agenda and/or make it a collaborative decision among the attendees.

Tip #21. What To Do When Your Content Exists as a Text (Word Processed) Document File or PDF

When in a situation where your content is in a text file or PDF (portable document format) and you have no time or no interest in putting it into a presentation format, here's what to do. No sweat.

During the Web Conference, use an Application Sharing / Application Viewing feature to show the content on your computer screen. Change the view (e.g. from 75% to 150%) to make the text appear larger.

With word processed documents, do additional things, before the Web Conference or on-the-fly, such as:

- Open the text file and save it with a new name.
- For the content you want to show everyone, make the font larger and if possible delete (cut) text that is not necessary.
- Use color for headings and key points.
- Change the Left/Right margin to 2" on each side.

Tip #22. Create Presentation Slides with Space for Annotations

When using presentation slides where your Web Conference objectives includes a lot of collaborative activity (e.g. brainstorming, eliciting ideas and comments, and one person building on what another person says), create the presentation slides so there is a lot of room to annotate them, by adding new text to the screens.

This technique allows participants to easily see ideas and comments being put forth. You can "screen capture" the annotated slides and save them for future use and/or for immediately distribution to participants.

On the next page are two examples of slide formats that allow for easy annotation during a Web Conferences. Experiment to see what works best for you.

Presentation Slides – with room for annotation

Agenda

Attendees

Portal Discussion

Support Services

Who Can Access

How would you use New Time?

Work?

Time at Home?

Tip #23. What To Do When Web Conferencing Software Does Not Have the Poll / Survey Feature

Here's a workaround you may be able to do with your Web Conferencing software. Show a presentation slide and have participants place a checkmark, star, or other annotation symbol next to an item. For example, you could put up a slide with two words, Yes and No. Frame your verbal question so the participants put their star or checkmark next to either Yes or No.

Here's another technique. Suppose you have a ten-person meeting. With the presentation slide showing, ask individuals to place a checkmark or star next to the sentence they agreement with. If you get all nine checkmarks, then you'll know everyone is in agreement. If only five checkmarks show, you'll know roughly half the audience is in agreement with that point.

Tip #24. Stay Organized with Your Questions

Here are two ideas for keeping track of questions you prepare ahead of time.

- Write your questions on 3x5 cards and keep these near you. If needed, tape these cards to your computer's monitor.
- Create a text document with questions in 16 point font. Print and keep the document in front of you. Use a highlighter pen for emphasis. Divvy up the questions to others on the team, so it's not just you asking questions.

Tip #25. Print and Refer to Your Slide Deck

If you are using a presentation slide deck, print the deck and place it into a 3-ring binder. (1) Type your questions for each slide into the "speaker notes" and print them. (2) Or, print the file and place the pages into the binder. Then, handwrite your questions on the blank left pages. Make sure the right side slide corresponds to the question(s) on the left side. It's like having a book, with questions on the left side and the slides on the right side.

Tip #26. Use Humor

Humor is powerful in Web Conferences. It can reinforce a learning point (which helps to increase retention), increase acceptance of a difficult message, warm up an audience, and decrease the stress that is sometimes associated with a very serious subject. Here are a few ideas: (1) Use a humorous image or chart in contrast to your serious images and charts. (2) Add a picture of you or your co-presenter – at age 3 or 10. (3) Use and discuss a humorous quotation, such as a quote from a popular book author, television personality, or sports figure.

Tip #27. Loosen Up

If you've been sitting for hours at your desk, extraordinarily focused in writing a document and working hard, and you have not even been on the phone, consider taking a moment to relax your body and loosen up your vocal chords before the Web Conference.

- Stretch your muscles – neck, shoulder, and legs. Yep, stand-up, move around and get your blood circulating.

- Warm up your vocal chords. Practice your volume (soft, loud) and your pace (slow, fast). Loosen up your vocal chords by using your voice to go up and down a music scale (do-re-mi-fa-so-lah-ti-do). (You can also encourage the participants to do this exercise.)

Tip #28. Remember, a Web Conference is Not Television

Television is a medium where it seems people are always talking. I have facilitated and attended Web Conferences where we had pauses and silence. Why were there pauses? People were thinking before they spoke. As someone once said, "*We need more listening and thinking and less talking.*"

Another point to remember is Web Conferencing is "interactive;" television is not.

Tip #29. Assign a Time (Agenda) Keeper

Assign someone to be the time/agenda-keeper. This person will help keep the meeting to the announced time. If you think you will go over the scheduled time, ask the group what to do. They may vote to extend the Web Conference for a longer period of time, or they may want to look at their calendars and book another time.

Tip #30. Control Your Stress by using Positive Self-Talk and Good Preparation

With traditional face-to-face situations, there are times when I show up to lead a workshop, a meeting or conference, feeling a certain amount of stress. At the same time I'm running these questions in my mind:

- *Will I be able to successfully connect my laptop to the projection system, so I don't get that blank "No Signal" screen?*
- *Will the LAN port work and take me out to the Internet*
- *Will the password(s) given to me work for getting to the intranet?*
- *Will the microphone system work?*

> The types of stress I sometimes feel with a face-to-face meeting or workshop is similar to the feelings I had as a Web Conferencing Beginning Presenter. It's also a type of stress I feel when I'm in charge of a very important or large Web Conference.

Positive Self-Talk: For me, using positive self-talk is the antidote to any stress I might be feeling. I use the following self-talk phrases to keep my mind positive:

"I can do this"
"It's not what happens that affects my emotional well-being, it's how I handle it that matters."

Good Preparation: As a former Boy Scout, I try to practice their motto of "Be Prepared." Before the Web Conference, I (or my staff) communicate special needs to the appropriate Web Conferencing Leader, Coordinator, and Technical Support Persons.

On the day of the Web Conference, when I am leading, I build in a few minutes of extra time before it starts. This gives me time to pause and relax.

I also have cell phone numbers, pager numbers, instant messenger (IM) addresses, and e-mail addresses of people who can help if there are any "technical difficulties."

Building Relationships

The tips and techniques give ideas for building relationships and creating a positive experience for people new to Web Conferencing.

Tip #31. Leader - Make a Warm-Up Telephone Call

When you are the Web Conference Leader, telephone and/or e-mail participants before the Web Conference. Help these "new people" warm up to this technology.

Tip #32. Assist with the Computer's System Check

If you are the person in the Web Conference Coordinator or Technical Support role, arrange a time with the participant several days before the Web Conference. In a brief five minute telephone meeting, you can assist the person with the Web Conference computer's system check.

Tip #33. Use a Greeter and Allocate Practice Time

When you go to a public seminar or event, you are usually greeted with a friendly face and smile. Do the same with Web Conferences. Arrange for the Web Conference to be "open" 15-30 minutes before the actual time. Invite participants to enter the Web Conference early so they can socialize with the "greeter" and others who come early.

- If you have people new to Web Conferencing, use this time to practice some of the interaction and annotation tools. For example, demonstrate how to use text chat and other features.

Tip #34. Inform Others When You Can't Attend the Web Conference

If you called the meeting, but can not attend and if there are new people who need to be introduced, assign someone to take on that responsibility and provide them with "bio's" (unless you use a more informal process).

Tip #35. Chit-Chat / Small Talk

Web Conferences, like face-to-face meetings, are about people. This means the Web Conference is a social experience. For Web Conferences where people do not know each other, take a few minutes to socialize your audience, talk sports, restaurants, family, food recipes, and so forth. Of course, if your participants are the "get down to business" type, you need to remember that as well.

Tip #36. Personalize with Pictures

When participants have not met face-to-face, I invite them to send me a picture of themselves. Then, I show the pictures during a Web Conference. If you use co-presenters, introduce them with their picture. "App share" (Application Sharing) pictures or insert them into a presentation slide.

Tip #37. Use Ice-Breakers to Warm-Up the Audience

Remember the fun, team-building games we play during offsite conferences. Here are a few possibilities for use during Web Conferences, but feel free to add your own:

- Show pictures of people outside of work, golfing, cooking, bicycling, dancing, with family, and so forth.
- Show baby pictures of participants. Play a game to see who can recognize the baby pictures.
- Show pictures of people that have been "morphed."

Tip #38. Know Country Holidays with International Web Conferences

Allan Austin offers the suggestion of using an international time zone and holiday software utility to help build rapport. He says it is valuable to know how a Web Conference "date" might coincide or interfere with a national holiday. He uses software called "ZoneTrekker."

Engaging and Involving Participants

These tips and techniques give ideas on how to engage and involve participants.

Tip #39. Obtain Management Support When There is a Pre-Web Conference Requirement

Obtain management support to help ensure participants complete any "pre-work." Otherwise; the work may not get done. Some organizations even give out small prizes as incentives for those who complete the assignment.

Tip #40. During the Web Conference, Remind Participants to "Announce" their Name When Speaking

This is important if the Web Conferencing system does not show the names and also when participants are joining for "audio" only.

Tip #41. Demonstrate (Model) and Encourage "Active Listening"

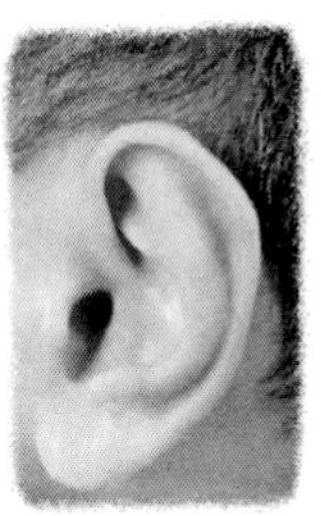

"Active Listening" is important for teams/people who come together to perform in a collaborative manner. Active Listening behavior includes:

- Concentrate on the speaker,
- Pay attention to the information, i.e. what is said, how it is said, and what is not said.
- Focus on the information vs. your questions-reactions-responses or rebuttal.
- Ask questions to clarify your interpretation of what was said.
- Restate what you think you heard.
- Do not dismiss the speaker or the information.
- Limit the arguments and questions asked of the speaker.

- Participate in a way that builds a sense of mutual cooperation, particularly when you disagree.

I have facilitated Web Conferences when participation was on the low side because of reasons such as: low trust among the group or there was a perception of loss of power by sharing knowledge. I have also facilitated teams when the consensus-building and decision-making was strong, but it turned out to be phony. The reason is few were committed to following-through on what they said they would do.

Tip #42. Use Questions to Involve

Before a Web Conference, prepare your approach and questions to keep people engaged, involved, and thinking. Although important for face-to-face meetings, it is especially important for Web Conferencing because you can not observe everyone's body language. (Looking at Chapter 1, Examples 1-5 through 1-10, if you are the Presenter in one of the conference rooms, you are able to see the body language of these people.)

I have facilitated Web Conferences where I planned ahead and did the right things. Everyone participated, even the so-called quiet ones. It's as if the Web Conference format makes things more democratic and participatory.

Once I had prepared a lot of questions, but I did not need them because of Dave. Dave was a peer of the regional managers. He had a style of stirring thing up (in a good way) by asking the hard questions, putting the issues right out on the table, putting others on the spot, and challenging those who shied away from giving their opinions. Based on the purpose of the meeting, Dave was darn appropriate.

And yet, with any Web Conference, the quantity and quality of participating may have less to do with your skills and more to do with the participants and the culture in which they work. For example, I have facilitated Web Conferences when relatively few people participated. I discovered, too late, that the participants did not participate much because they were waiting to hear what the boss was going to say.

Tip #43. Use Open-Ended and Closed Questions

Generally, these elicit more detail in a person's response. (Sometimes, you need to give a long pause before someone breaks the ice.)

- *How is the audio?*
- *What would you like to add? What ideas do you have?*
- *Regarding this last part of the discussion, what parts do you agree with? (Disagree with?)*
- *What are some of the options you envision?*
- *What steps would you take in dealing with this situation?*
- *From your point of view, what is the upside of Mike's suggestion?*
- *What do you think needs to be done to support Mike's suggestion?*
- *When you think about Lisa's ideas, what else comes to mind?*
- *Jane, if you accept Mike's suggestion, what impacts will that have on your organization? Bob, now that you've heard from Mike and Jane, what are your thoughts?*
- *What factors will impact hitting the target date? What factors do you think will impede our progress? What can we do to accelerate our progress? What factors will propel us toward achieving the goal?*
- *What concerns do you have with the proposed plan?*

Close-Ended Questions: Generally, these elicit "yes" or "no" responses. Sometimes, people talk past these questions and give a meaty response.

- *Can you see the visuals on your screen?*
- *Does everyone understand?*
- *Do you have any questions?*
- *Did you read the report before the Web Conference*
- *Will you give an example?*
- *Do you agree with Mike's suggestions?*
- *Do you think we can meet the target date?*

Tip #44. Are You "Going After" Passive or Active Involvement?

When designing your Web Conference and planning your questions, it helps to think about your questions from the perspectives of "passive" vs. "active involvement."

Passive Involvement of Participants – Question Examples: As you see, the following questions are Close-Ended.

- *Does everyone understand?*
- *Are there any questions?*
- *Do you agree?*
- *Do you disagree?*
- *How many of you like this? Raise your hand.*

Active Involvement of Participants – Question Examples: These questions provide more direction and generally elicit more meat in the response.

- *Bill, will you please restate in your words what Mary has been saying? I want to make sure we're on the same page.*
- *Who will summarize what we've been talking about? Okay, what's your summary?*
- *Suppose you are the finance director, what are some of the concerns you might have about this proposal?*

Tip #45. Engage the People to Solve a Problem or to "Go After" an Opportunity

If you want to put your participants to sleep, merely talk about a problem or opportunity for thirty minutes or so. Very boring!

- **Questions**: Rather than "telling" participants your perception of the *problem* or *opportunity*, I suggest you engage the people by "asking questions." Give enough information, and then have them react to the information. Someone can type the responses on the computer screen, if appropriate.
- **Case Study**: Another technique is to show a case study or organizational situation to participants. Then, get their reactions and ideas about it.
- **Role Play**: With very little preparation and on-the-fly, you can execute a role play. For example, ask George to speak as if he is the citizen; ask Joel to speak as if he is the elected official; and ask Ellen to speak as if she is the department head. Facilitate a discussion based on what they are saying to each other about the problem.

Tip #46. Achieve the Group Conversation (Group Dialogue)

Sometimes, my objective is have participants engage each other rather than engaging me. I think of this as a group or team conversation or dialogue. At times, participants seize the moment and engage each other with very little prodding or facilitation from me.

Sometimes I need to drive participants to engage each other. I strive to use Active Listening techniques and I try to build off each person's responses. Here is an example of how I accomplish this.

- Ask a question of Jim. Wait for a response.
- Restate your understanding of Jim's response and have him acknowledge you understood his point.
- Then ask a question of Mary, that pivots off Jim's response and your first question to Jim. Wait for a response.
- Ask a participant to restate what they think they heard Mary say.
- Then ask a question back to Jim or ask a question of another participant, to get them involved. Try to build off other peoples' responses with your questions.

Tip #47. Check for Language

How do you know if the language you use is in synchronization with the needs of your audience? Here are several things you can do during the Web Conference.

Define jargon: Take a moment to define new terms (jargon).

Check for understanding. Check for understanding and give participants an opportunity for clarification.

- *"Raise your hand if I use a term you are not sure about."*
- *"Send me a text message if I use any fifty-cent words."*
- *"Annotate the screen with a checkmark if I start using jargon that is unfamiliar to you."*

Developing Your Web Conferencing Skills

Tip #48. Make Commitment to Learn and Practice

Open up your calendar and schedule a meeting with yourself. Use your scheduled time to learn and practice.

Tip #49. Know the Web Conferencing Features

Become familiar with the features your Web Conference software or system provides.

Tip #50. Learn Tips and Techniques from Others

Communicate with people who have experience with Web Conferencing – users and technical folks. Find out their "tips and techniques." Observe others who lead Web Conferencing virtual meetings and training sessions.

Tip #51. List Your Desired Web Conferencing Skills

Write an initial list of what you want to learn and use. Then, work through your list. Here's an example initial list.

- ❑ Schedule the Web Conference
- ❑ Send out invitations
- ❑ Show a slide presentation
- ❑ Mark up a slide presentation (checkmark, highlighter)
- ❑ Show a survey or poll
- ❑ Show a text document or spreadsheet and make changes to it during the Web Conference
- ❑ Have everyone see a web site at the same time
- ❑ Send and save chat messages
- ❑ Send a file to participants during the Web Conference
- ❑ Coordinate the audio (voice) part of the Web Conference

Tip #52. Avoid Feeling Overwhelmed

Web Conferencing software is pretty darn powerful. Some vendors offer a great number of features and capabilities, which you may or may not need.

I know some people new to Web Conferencing feel overwhelmed when they try to learn and practice "everything" at once. If you are told in the beginning, there are fifteen or twenty fantastic tools; I strongly suggest you get comfortable with just a few features (skills) at a time.

Tip #53. Use Job Aids Provided by Your Web Conferencing Software Vendor

Print out and use job aids provided by the Web Conferencing software company. Refer to these job aids as you practice using the software. If job aids do not exist, ask your vendor and technical staff to prepare some for you.

Tip #54. Practice and Get Feedback

Give a practice session and have someone you rely on, critique the session. Hopefully, that person has experience with Toastmasters®. When Toastmasters® give feedback, it is usually enthusiastic and positive in tone, and includes what you did right as well as what areas can be improved.

Tip #55. Start Small, Think Big

As a presenter, start with a light Web Conference of thirty to sixty minutes with your team or peers. When I first started out, I asked friends, relatives, and peers if we could try it out in off-hours. Most of them were very receptive because they also wanted to learn more about this method for getting people together.

Tip #56. Build Your Skills, Comfort, and Confidence through Repetition

If you want to be smooth with a particular skill (See Tip #51), practice the skill 5-10 times. Use any job aids available and practice. Once in the groove, the skill will be second nature to you.

Tip #57. Practice Your Timing

Use a watch when you go through your presentation and jot down how much time you spend on each slide. Or, use the "rehearse timings" feature in your slide show program. When feasible, another option is to simulate the meeting with another person. Have this person keep notes on your timing.

If you plan for a good amount of collaborative discussion and Q&A, remember this when you gauge the length of your Web Conference.

Tip #58. Create Your Own Customized Job Aids

After you gain familiarity with the Web Conferencing software, consider making your own job aids. You might want a customized reminder system. Do you ever watch the football coaches on television? The camera often shows them referring to their laminated job aid of what plays to call.

It is easy and fast to jot down the things you want to remember (e.g. key strokes and key stroke sequences) during a Web Conferencing.

Another approach is to type up and print your reminders and staple them to other sheets you have already printed.

Tip #59. Practice "Seeing" a Web Conference in Action

This technique has been very helpful to me. Since starting out with Web Conferencing, I've used over a dozen different systems. This method helps me get a feel for each system and how their features operate.

The following techniques have built my confidence and given me a type of "empathy" for other people. In other words, I see the Web Conference from the participant's point of view. I found this empowering.

Position two computers side-by-side, each connected to the web. Setup a Web Conference practice session, or have someone else set it up. (A) On one of the computer's, dial into the Web Conference session as a "presenter." (B) On the other computer, dial into the Web Conference session as a "participant" or "guest."

A. Login as Presenter

B. Login as Participant or Guest

You see the same thing on both monitors.

At the computer where you have signed on as "presenter," work the features (e.g. show a web site, show and markup a presentation slide). Watch each computer's screen to see how each screen changes and looks.

At the computer where you have signed on as a "participant" or "guests," perform different tasks (chat message, raise hand, place a checkmark on a slide, etc.). Again, watch each computer's screen to see how each screen changes and looks.

Tip #60. Stay Organized When Using Multiple Files During a Web Conference

If you plan to use a number of different files during the same Web Conference, consider copying them into a new folder before the meeting. You might find having them in one place is helpful to you.

I've been in situations where I've had to search my hard drive for a file. It took longer than I wanted, but no one complained. In fact, several of the participants struck up a conversation and one said everyone needed a break anyway. I don't know if she was kidding or not, but it caused everyone to laugh.

Tip #61. Do You Like to Stand During the Web Conference?

If you wear a headset, you may already know that an extension cord gives you a little more freedom. If you use a headset and you like to stand up while leading a Web Conference, buy an inexpensive extension cord so you can move around during the Web Conference. Of course, you want to see the computer monitor and be close to the keyboard.

If you are in a single-office, and don't want to wear a headset, use an external microphone and speakers. This also gives you some flexibility.

Extra Tips

Tip #62. How To Protect Your Webcam and Headset When Traveling

These are fragile, valuable items. Consider protecting them by wrapping these items in bubble pack and inserting into a zippered food storage bag.

Tip #63. Be Creative in Choosing Where You Connect From

I co-facilitated a meeting where the other facilitator, Allan Austin, was on a cruise ship,. He was on vacation and did not want to miss the Web Conference. Although his connection was a little pricey, the Web Conference met its objectives and more. The participants were amazed Allan was in the middle of the ocean.

You may be able to participate from someone else's computer, in their office. Ahead of time, double-check with your Web Conferencing Coordinator to see how to make it work.

Tip #64. Will You Become a Web Conference Power User?

If your plan is to become a power user of Web Conferencing software, here are several suggestions.

- Keep practicing.

- Print out the Web Conferencing Help files and Job Aids. Place them into a 3-ring binder or have them spiral bound. Carry the binder in your briefcase and read and highlight appropriate sections.

- **Find a Technical Coach**: Find a person who can be your Web Conferencing technical coach. Tell your technical coach what you want to accomplish in using Web Conferencing and listen to other ideas that might make your Web Conferences even better. Invite this person to supplement what you already know and can do.

For example, the technical coach may have special techniques for uploading files, the best way to advance slides, how to create and use a poll or survey, and what buttons to click on with your mouse.

- **Organizational Development (OD) Coach**: Find a person who can be your "organizational development" coach. A person with OD skills usually very good at understanding group dynamics, change management, and facilitating discussions. These skills are very helpful when your objectives include increasing the quality and quantity of communication, cooperation, and collaboration in a group or team. If the lack of trust is an issue for the group or team, an OD coach is a good person to help you. If, on the other hand, your group or team is well-functioning, or if you mostly use Web Conferencing to disseminate information, you probably don't need an OD coach.

Tip #65. Health Promotion

Here are several tips, some from OSHA (Occupational and Safety and Health Administration, U.S. Government) and NIOSH (National Institute for Occupational Safety and Health, U.S. Government).

- **Breaks**: Take periodic breaks, e.g. a 10-minute break after two hours of continuous computer work.

- **Rest Your Eyes**: In between breaks, decrease eye strain by looking away from the computer screen. Look at objects about 20 feet away.

- **Stretch Your Hands and Fingers**: Periodically, open and close your hands.

- **Take A Walk**: If you are traveling less and have New Time (pages 43 and 44), use some of this time for walking and exercise.

Notes

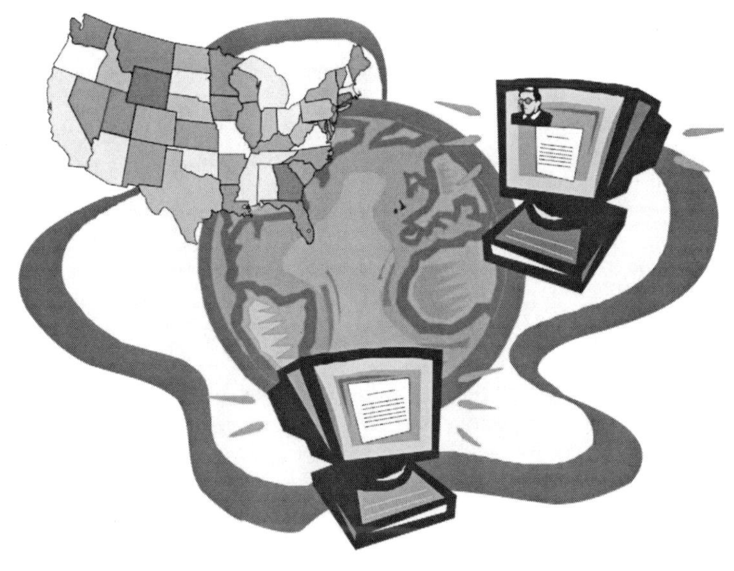

Appendix

Personal Assessment

New Time Management (see pages 43 and 44)

How might you use *your* New Time?

- ☐ Work
- ☐ Family
- ☐ Sports, Exercise, Cooking, Socializing
- ☐ Volunteering
- ☐ Learning
- ☐ Sleeping
- ☐ Television
- ☐ I have no earthly idea
- ☐ Other ______________________

What interests you about using Web Conferencing? *Check all that may apply*.

Day-To-Day

- ☐ Leading and participating in Web Conferences from home, hotel, and other locations
- ☐ Highly interactive, engaging, and collaborative meetings
- ☐ Co-creating
- ☐ Presentations to large audiences, using individual PCs, projection systems, and electronic whiteboards
- ☐ Thorough discussions and faster agreement on a project's definition, scope, and plan
- ☐ Virtual organizational development interventions
- ☐ Agreement on issues, proposed solutions, and coordination among people in multiple locations
- ☐ Virtual meetings with peers, staff, and team members
- ☐ Managing internal and external business relationships
- ☐ Being on the same page with suppliers and partners
- ☐ Follow-up after face-to-face meetings
- ☐ Becoming a Great Web Conferencing Communicator

Training and Workforce Performance

- ☐ Deployment of "same time" (synchronous) learning for courses, classes, and follow-up sessions
- ☐ Blended Learning opportunities
- ☐ Becoming Great at Instructional Design, Course Development, and Virtual Instruction (Facilitation)